Chaoxianzu Entrepreneurs in Korea

This book explores the nature of the state-citizen societal relationship in Korea during the transition to neoliberalism, through the lenses of class and nationalism.

Examining the process by which a new class, Korean Chinese entrepreneurs, emerged from Korean Chinese enclaves in South Korea and quickly became a leading group within those communities, this book provides a case study of the entrepreneurs running a variety of businesses, including restaurants, travel agencies and trading companies. Whilst Korean Chinese people faced discrimination and stigmatization in Korea, despite their economic contributions to the economy, this book demonstrates how entrepreneurs began to form associations and organisations, campaigning for their equal status in Korean society. Arguing that the formation of these was closely linked to the framework of legal statuses established by the Korean state as it sought to make use of Korean Chinese labour, this book explains how social citizenship was constituted by the interaction between their situational sense of fairness and the contradictory economic and social roles expected of them by the state.

Drawing on fifteen years of ethnographical experience, *Chaoxianzu Entrepreneurs in Korea* will be useful to students and scholars of sociology, anthropology, Migration Studies and Ethnic Studies, as well as Korean Studies.

Woo Park is Assistant Professor in the Department of Liberal Art and Science at Hansung University, South Korea. He studied at Yanbian University in China and received his MA and Ph.D. in sociology from Seoul National University.

Routledge Focus on Asia

Chaoxianzu Entrepreneurs in Korea

Searching for Citizenship in the Ethnic Homeland

Woo Park

Routledge
Taylor & Francis Group

LONDON AND NEW YORK

First published 2020
by Routledge
2 Park Square, Milton Park, Abingdon, Oxon OX14 4RN

and by Routledge
605 Third Avenue, New York, NY 10017

First issued in paperback 2021

Routledge is an imprint of the Taylor & Francis Group, an informa business

Publisher's Note
The publisher has gone to great lengths to ensure the quality of this reprint
but points out that some imperfections in the original copies may be
apparent.

British Library Cataloguing-in-Publication Data
A catalogue record for this book is available from the British Library

Library of Congress Cataloging-in-Publication Data
A catalog record has been requested for this book

ISBN 13: 978-1-03-223869-2 (pbk)
ISBN 13: 978-0-367-90076-2 (hbk)

Typeset in Times New Roman
by codeMantra

For my lovely family

Contents

Tables

Preface

Since 2000, South Korea has started to become a so-called "multicultural" society. One part of this phenomenon was the Korean Chinese, who are ethnically Korean but embodied Chinese culture. The Korean Chinese formed a kind of enclave in the Southwest Seoul that became the centre of their socio-economic life. As the Korean Chinese population grew, the community experienced economic differentiation. Korean Chinese enclave entrepreneurs emerged from a community of Korean Chinese migrant workers. These entrepreneurs ran a variety of businesses, including restaurants, travel agencies, and trading companies.

I have 15 years of ethnographical experience in this field. Since 2005 (based on my fieldwork), I have identified the formation of a new class in South Korea made up of Korean Chinese entrepreneurs. This is a very interesting phenomenon – an immigrant (or the returnee) petty bourgeoisie class emerging in a late-capitalist (or neo-liberal) economy. Korean Chinese people faced discrimination and stigmatization in Korea despite their economic contributions to the Korean economy, but the entrepreneurs began to form associations and organizations which campaigned for equal status in Korean society. How was this possible, and what sociological (or social scientific) implications can be revealed through this phenomenon? This book aims to characterize citizenship in South Korea with the help of two classical variables of social science, class and nationalism (ethnicity), both of which were key to the relationship between the South Korean state and the Korean Chinese entrepreneurs during the neo-liberal transformation.

In preparing the current book, I received tremendous intellectual support from Professor Chang Kyung-Sup. His book *South Korea under Compressed Modernity: Familial Political Economy in Transition* (2010), which systematically conceptualized the East Asian modernity, had the biggest impact on me. Also, when I was an assistant in the Institute for Social Development and Policy Research in Seoul National University, the ISDPR hosted an international conference and the articles of the conference were published as an academic book titled *Contested Citizenship in East Asia: Developmental Politics, National Unity, and Globalization* (2012), edited by Chang Kyung-Sup and Bryan S. Turner. As an assistant, it was an honour to learn a lot from the contributors. In recent years, *South Korea in Transition: Politics and Culture of Citizenship* (2014), which collects research on the characteristic of citizenship in South Korea in one volume, was also a very important influence. In 2018, I had the priceless opportunity to attend an international conference on *Developmental Citizenship(s) in China: Social Governance and Developmental Politics in Citizenship Perspective*, held at Seoul National University. This conference and its attendees helped me to understand aspects of China's citizenship regime. Having learned from many of the scholars mentioned above, I determined that I could do research people moving between Korea and China (even within East Asia). This phenomenon can be termed the "Asianization of Asia".

My colleague Robert Easthope was in charge of editing and correcting the manuscript and making it publishable. Lucid comment and suggestions offered by peer reviewers made the theoretical implications and limitations of the proposed manuscript much clearer. Also, the kind and friendly guidance of Routledge's Stephanie Rogers and Georgina Bishop was essential to publish the work as a book. Finally, I was able to complete this book thanks to the excellent research environment provided by Hansung University.

My wife, Rany, and my son, Justin, are the spiritual pillars supporting my research. To them, I dedicate this book.

Abbreviations

2008FSSVES	2008 Factual Survey on the Satisfaction of Visiting and Employment System
2008SKCE	2008 Survey on the Korean Chinese Enclave
2013SBG	2013 Survey on the Business of Garibong-dong
2013SKCLS	2013 Survey of Korean Chinese Living in Seoul
AILOK	Act on the Immigration and Legal Status of Overseas Korean
CKCA	Central Korean Chinese Assembly
EMS	Employment and Management System
EPS	Employment Permit System
FLEA	Foreign Laborer Employment Act
FLPC	Foreign Laborer Policy Committee
GAKCA	General Assembly of Korean Compatriots' Association
GIC	Guro Industrial Complex
GPC	Globalization Promotion Committee
ICA	Immigration Control Act
ITTS	Industrial Technical Training System
KCA	Korean Chinese Association
KCC	Korean Chinese Committee
KCEMA	Korea-China Entrepreneurship and Management Association
KCMA	Korean Compatriot Merchant Association
KCN	Korean Chinese Students Network
KCTA	Korea-China Trade Association
KCTN	Korean Chinese Town Newspaper
KCWMC	Korean Chinese Welfare Mission Centre
KDWP	Korean Diplomatic White Paper
KEF	Korea Employers Federation
KFSMB	Korea Federation of Small and Medium Business

KISS	Korean Immigration Service Statistic
KRA	Korean Returnees' Association
MCI	Ministry of Commerce and Industry
MOJ	Ministry of Justice
MOL	Ministry of Labor
OGPC	Office for Government Policy Coordination
OKF	Overseas Korean Foundation
OKFA	Overseas Korean Foundation Act
SMBA	Small and Medium Business Administration
TES	Training and Employment System
UAKC	United Association of Korean Chinese
UVS	United Volunteer Service
VES	Visiting and Employment System

1 Introduction

Localization of social citizenship

Between the late 1800s and late 1940s, particularly during the colonization of Korea by Imperial Japan, a considerable number of Koreans moved to Manchuria. They moved for a variety of reasons, some to take part in Korea's independence movement, some for missionary work, and others for business or employment. And when Manchuria became a part of the People's Republic of China, some of this population moved back to the Korean Peninsula. A large number, however, stayed and became Chinese nationals (Park 2017a, 2018, 2019). This book will refer to these people as Korean Chinese. They are called *Chaoxianzu* in Chinese and *Joseonjok* in Korea.

In the late 1980s, large numbers of this Korean Chinese population began to move from China to South Korea. It was a rapid process: while before 1987 there were less than 1,000 Korean Chinese visitors to Korea a year (Ministry of Foreign Affairs 1991: 218), by 2015 the number of Korean Chinese living in South Korea reached 618,673 (Korean Immigration Service 2016). This is a number similar to the population of Yanji (or Yeongil), the capital of China's Yanbian (Yeonbyeon) Korean Autonomous Prefecture. It is also about one-third the size of the Korean Chinese population in China (1,830,929, according to the 2010 Chinese census, China Statistical Yearbook 2010). This migration was driven, on the one hand, by a shortage of blue-collar labour in South Korea created when its economic structure began to transform in the 1980s (Seol 1999), and on the other, by the decline in socio-economic status experienced by some Korean Chinese in the wake of China's rapid transition away from socialism (Park 2017a). Later, in the 1990s, institutions like the Overseas Korean Foundation (OKF) and laws like the Overseas Korean Act established a relationship of interdependence between South Korea and overseas Koreans, and a variety of complicated legal statuses were established for those with Korean heritage wishing to work or live in Korea (Park 2012; Park and Kim et al. 2012).

Southwest Seoul became the centre for this influx, and the Korean Export Industry Complex located there can be seen as a kind of historical theatre for South Korea's rapid process of industrialization, democratization, and urbanization.

The early inflow of migrants was sporadic, small in scale, and saw Korean Chinese moving to various parts of Seoul. From the 2000s, however, the Korean Chinese migrants began to cluster around Guro Digital Complex subway station: in 2007, there were 127,240 Korean Chinese living in Seoul, of whom 17,948 lived in Guro-gu ("gu" meaning administrative district of Metropolitan Seoul City). But by the end of 2015, there were 232,456 Korean Chinese in Seoul, with 41,117 in the Guro-gu. Yeongdeungpo-gu also saw its population of Korean Chinese rise from 21,907 to 50,964 over the same period. In Geumcheon-gu, the Korean Chinese population rose from 10,569 to 23,508, while in Gwanak-gu, it went from 10,908 to 21,352 (Korean Immigration Service 2008, 2016). Overall, by the end of 2015, 59.8% of Seoul's Korean Chinese population lived in southwest Seoul.

There is no evidence that when the South Korean government and capital were trying to incorporate Korean Chinese into the domestic labour market, they planned to establish any kind of enclave or encourage the emergence of entrepreneurs. However, the increase in the number Korean Chinese in this region created an opening for businesses able to serve the needs of this new, and growing, community. Entrepreneurs hired labour and opened a variety of businesses in food, retail, travel, and sales industries. This involved various forms of employment, including self-employment and family employment as well as salaried workers. Soon, in some parts of the region, over half of all businesses were owned by Korean Chinese or Korean Chinese who had acquired South Korean nationality.

Most of these people originally came to South Korea to work in the secondary labour market with an Overseas Korean visa or through visa policies aimed at attracting industrial manpower. It was only with the change in government policies and the formation of the Korean Chinese enclave that they began to make use of their various forms of capital to set up businesses. However, the entrepreneurs were not only engaged in profit creation – but also sought to lead public opinion and represent the area, establishing organizations (associations) and becoming involved in various projects and activities. They tried to use their status as entrepreneurs to become equal members of Korean society through the acquisition of citizenship status.

This emerging (petit bourgeoisie) class of Korean Chinese entrepreneurs can help us to understand and explain the characteristics
of state-citizen(ship) relations in neo-liberal transitional periods. We
should ask how the Korean Chinese entrepreneur class emerged, what
the logic was behind their citizenship practice, and how the localization of their social citizenship was structured.

With that in mind, this book will first describe the system of legal
statuses in South Korea that had a decisive influence on the class's
emergence. Second, it will discuss the enclave market, which was one
of the determinants of the entrepreneurs' class position. Third, it will
explore how the interaction between legal status and resources (or
market) gave rise to this class. Fourth, it will analyze the aspects and
reasons for the entrepreneurs' citizenship *practices*. Lastly, it will analyze the diverse roles as the entrepreneurs given to them by the South
Korean state and society.

Existing studies of South Korea's Korean Chinese

Although there has never before been an academic analysis of Korean
Chinese entrepreneurs' emergence as a significant group, or their attempt to secure membership in South Korean society, there has been
extensive research into the Korean Chinese community and immigration in general in South Korea. We can divide the scholars interested in this area into two groups: those concerned with the group's
categorization and those who analyze its role in providing a pool of
immigrant labour. Within the first group, there are scholars drawn
to practical questions about how the state should be dealing with the
Korean Chinese. Some like Lee (2001) and Loh (1999, 2002) argue
that the Korean Chinese need to be legally categorized as Overseas
Korean (*jaeoedongpo*), while others like Jung (1999) and Park (2001)
argue that the Korean Chinese should be categorized as normal immigrants but with their special cultural and ethnic characteristics
taken into extra consideration because a state applying regulation
to another state's citizens based on ideas of blood and descent could
cause diplomatic conflict (Lee 2002). There are also scholars interested in the way the Korean Chinese's ethnic identity is reflected in
the legislation process (Kim 2016). These approaches are related to
a perspective from which the Korean Chinese are seen as part of the
Korean diaspora (Jung 2013).[1]

The second group (interested in the Korean Chinese's economic
role) argues that imported labour (including Korean Chinese) filled
the industrial jobs avoided by the domestic labour force (Lee 1994;

Lee et al. 1998; Seok et al. 2003) and was economically efficient. A part of the foundation of South Korea's economic development was the unskilled and low-paid workforce who endured discrimination in the secondary labour market. For these scholars, the industrial demand created the need for this labour, and the functional requirement decided Foreign Workers' legal status (or visa type) (Seol and Skrentny 2009; Seol 2012). From this study's perspective, as a foreign industrial labour force with limited economic autonomy who could only be integrated into specific, low-wage industries, it was inevitable that Korean Chinese would become a lower economic class group in South Korea and that their residential area would become ghettoized or become a slum.

Defining Korean Chinese entrepreneurs

The term Korean Chinese refers to a group of Koreans and their descendants who left the Korean Peninsula and moved to China in the first half of the 20th century. "Korean Chinese" is not an academic concept. Since the *Minzu* (nationalities) policy in the early 1950s conducted by the Government of the People's Republic of China, the communist China recognized Chinese citizenship for Koreans who were living in China, and the Koreans became one of 56 *Minzu* in China. In this sense, Korean Chinese is an administrative or policy term composed of ethnic Koreans.

This population was composed of ethnic Koreans with Chinese citizenship and was dispersed over a large area covering the eastern part of the Inner Mongolia Autonomous Region and the three provinces of northeast China (Liaoning, Jilin, and Heilongjiang). As a result of China's reform and opening policy, the Korean Chinese people of this region experienced rapid differentiation and movement. About one-third of this population is now living in South Korea.

Some of the Korean Chinese in South Korea have acquired Korean nationality through a change in their legal status. These Korean citizens can no longer be considered to fall under the Chinese government's ethnic policy. However, Korean Chinese entrepreneurs emerged as an important group in an enclave where the majority of the Korean Chinese population had not acquired South Korean nationality, and their businesses cater to this group, and the majority of the network we are interested in is composed of Korean Chinese. So this book will use the term Korean Chinese regardless of nationality.

In sociology, actors who found companies after immigration have been called "immigrant entrepreneurs", and immigrant economies termed "ethnic economies" (Light and Sanchez 1987; Light and Bonacich 1988; Light and Karageorgis 1994; Light and Gold 2000, Light 2005). The term entrepreneur refers to a person who sets up a business and is in the position of the employer in an employment relationship. This includes self-employment, family employment, or paid employment.[2]

To summarize, the term "Korean Chinese entrepreneur" is used regardless of current nationality to refer to someone who (a) is currently or was in the past categorized by the Chinese government as Korean Chinese and (b) is the employer in an employment relationship.

Transformative citizenship

T. H. Marshall (1950) was the first to raise citizenship as a key concept of state-citizen relations in sociology. He was interested in how unequal social classes with different ideals, beliefs, and values could develop and maintain cooperative relations within one state. His work played a key role in expanding the idea of citizenship, previously the territory of political philosophy, into a sociological concept (Turner, 1986: 13–26). This allowed "citizenship" to become an important indicator for criticizing and assessing the character of modern (generally Western) societies (Turner 1990). It opened discussion of not only status and citizenship rights but also the history of social groups' public and conscious struggle for social participation (Turner 1986).

In order to address the issue of status, rights, and citizenship, Turner (1993: 2–3) defined citizenship as the result of a flow of goods and resources towards a people or a social group – with these groups being defined as an assemblage of juridical, political, economic, and cultural *practices*. From this perspective, citizenship regulates access to limited resources for individuals and groups in society. Rights and obligations are institutionalized in official statuses and allow for access to limited resources in formal societies. These resources can be economic, cultural, or political, and the rights to access such resources can be termed economic rights, cultural rights, and political rights, respectively: economic rights are related to basic needs such as food and housing; cultural rights to welfare and education; and political rights to traditional areas of liberalism, such as personal freedom and the right to political expression through democratic institutions. These rights are collectively termed "social" rights by Turner, differentiating them from human rights (Turner 1997: 5–9). Turner's concept of citizenship refers to a set of "contributory rights" and obligations situated within the framework of the nation-state relating to labour, public services (e.g. military, legal services), and parenting or family formation. Importantly, he argues that they are "contributory rights" because claims on a society are only effective if based on contributions – that is, if the claimants are supplying something that the society requires, such as participation in the labour market, the military, or social reproduction (Turner 2001; Isin and Turner 2007: 2, 12). According to Turner's logic, we can explain that the citizenship of modern individuals is based on the recognition that contributory rights are fairly distributed (or granted). This "sense of fairness" (identity) has served as a principle for individual citizenship practice.

The concept of citizenship used by Marshall (1950) helps to explain the relationship between the state and various social groups (as well as the citizen) as they emerged from a relatively long and stable modernization process and does so on the basis of Western rationality and individualism. However, this makes it difficult to apply the concept directly to areas that experienced quicker and more volatile modernization processes, like East Asia (Chang 2012a, 2012b). This means we need to modify the concepts of citizenship if it is to help us understand the state-citizen relationship in South Korea (Chang and Turner 2012; Turner and Chang 2012).

Chang's (2010: 5–8) theory of South Korean (and East Asia) society is useful here. His guiding concept is the notion of "compressed modernity". Compressed modernity draws attention to the complex relationship between modernity and Korea's traditional ideas and *practices*, which coexist thanks to its adoption of Western experience over just a few decades. This relationship is the cause and result of the political and economic transformations witnessed in Korea over the last century as well as the repeated reorganizations of its state-society relationship.

The content and nature of citizenship in Korean society was redefined at every moment of this political-economic transition. Institutional and techno-scientific modernization and educational citizenship, economic transformation and developmental citizenship, democratization and transformative political citizenship, globalization and neo-liberal versus cosmopolitan citizenship, national reconfiguration and compatriotic citizenship – all these relationships – were redefined. According to Chang, under this transformation, "There have arisen transformation-oriented state, society, and population for which each transformation becomes an ultimate purpose in itself, the process and means of the transformation constitute the main sociopolitical order, and the transformation-embedded interests form the core social identity" (Chang 2014).

Neo-liberalism demanded the transformation of a series of economic and political structures, including the labour market. This was pursued by the South Korean state and international order through the creation of a new ideology and policies designed to materially integrate citizens into public life (a project which was both possible and inevitable because of the weak state-citizen relationship). As such, the citizenship of Koreans came to be based not on firmly established rights, duties, and identities within a stable social system but rather on the basis of "contributions" that are subject to constant upheavals in state and society. From within these transformations always emerge social groups that are either excluded or oppressed (Chang and Tuner 2012; Chang 2012c).

The state-dominated globalization of Korea since the early 1990s did not begin of its own making but was made necessary by the political and economic context of neo-liberal globalization, and the transformations concerned have embodied various neo-liberal tendencies (Chang 2012b). A part of the logic of this globalization was institutionalized by a strategy which attempted to reinstate South Korea's past conditions of work and marriage through foreign bodies (Chang 2014: 172). One of the major targets of this economic (and industrial) development plan and strategy for social reproduction was the large number of foreign workers and brides from Asia who had been incorporated into the Korean society. The major part of this population is Korean Chinese, an extremely complex group whose ethnic identity and status as industrial workers are intricately intertwined (Park 2017b). Since the late 1980s and early 1990s, about 600,000 Korean Chinese have been incorporated into Korean society. This population is fragmented across the primary (Park 2013) and secondary labour market (Seol and Skrentny 2009; Seol 2012), as well as fulfils roles in social reproduction (Kim 2012, 2014). There are various paths and sets of qualifications through which they can become South Korean nationals (Lee 2012).[3]

Under the transformation-orientated logic of South Korean society, the rights and duties of new groups were defined according to the resources and contributions required by constantly evolving development goals. These selectively defined rights have been a key cause of the social and economic equality experienced by migrant groups in the midst of the ongoing political and economic change. At the same time, these social groups, who have been placed in an unequal structure, find themselves practicing citizenship on the basis of fairness.

We can thus define transformative citizenship (transformative contributory right) as "effective and/or legitimate claims to national and social resources, opportunities and/or respects and accrue to citizens' contributions to the nation's or society's transformative purpose" (Chang 2014: 164).

Method and materials

I encountered the Korean Chinese enclave in 2005 as a volunteer at a Korean Chinese Thanksgiving event in Guro's Garibong-dong area hosted by Korean Chinese Town Newspaper (KCTN) and Korean Chinese Students Network in Korea (KCN). The following year I served as a guest reporter for this same newspaper, a role that provided the opportunity to observe, record, and investigate the problems (large and small) that faced the enclave's residents. That summer the newspaper held a consultation on the government's voluntary departure policy for people staying illegally, and I began to understand more systematically the paths that brought Korean Chinese into the country and the visa (or legal) statuses they held.

These years were an important turning point for Korean Chinese in South Korea – changes to the Overseas Koreans Act in 2004 allowed Korean Chinese to live in South Korea with *either* a visiting work visa *or* an Overseas Korean visa from 2007. I was able to observe and record how unregistered Korean Chinese were leaving the country and then returning to South Korea with legitimate documents one or two years later. In one case I was involved more directly; Mr H from Hunchun in China's Jilin province went back to China in 2006 after consulting me. I saw him again two years later when he returned to South Korea on a visiting employment visa.

The visiting employment system changed the landscape of Korean Chinese society. The first thing an interested observer would have noticed was that there were simply more people on the streets of Garibong-dong, and they seemed to have a new air of dignity about them. The second thing they might have noticed was that organizations, both small and big, began to spring up like mushrooms. I was involved in the establishment of almost all these organizations and participated in most of their events, a relationship which has lasted until the present day. The third change our witness might have noticed was that "Daerim-dong" began to come up more in people's everyday conversations, and journalists even began to say that the "Daerim-dong era" has arrived. As a result of the large number of Korean Chinese population being incorporated into Korean society thanks to the implementation of the visiting employment system, the densely populated areas of Doksan-dong, Garibong-dong, and Guro-dong became saturated, and the Korean Chinese population expanded into nearby Daerim-dong.

Since 2009, I have been the core member of an association and, as a result, have been able to stay closer to the community and learn much about the history and structure of Korean Chinese organizations. These groups have been dominant in Korean Chinese areas since taking over from religious groups in the aftermath of the 2007 visa changes. They are competitive with each other, and quite a few of them have disappeared after struggling to keep up. The biggest and continually growing groups are all led by Korean Chinese Entrepreneurs. After the entrepreneurs who run the associations obtained legitimate residency in South Korea and became the legal owners of their businesses, they began to participate officially in social issues. I witnessed the emergence of an official Korean Chinese entrepreneur group and participated in the process by which these business people formed associations and began to fulfil roles in the local area.

From 2010 to the present day (2018), I observed the events not as a simple participant but as a researcher studying Korean Chinese society and enclaves. I often met with local businessmen who were steadily expanding the size of their own businesses and were looking to make the associations they run more formal. Public opinion in the dwelling was dominated by organizations run by entrepreneurs, and I was able to directly record the voices of the people who ran them. I was an advisor to one entrepreneurs' association, which allowed me to work with them more, particularly closely. I observed their efforts to become a formal part of South Korean society and the logic (identity) that lay behind those efforts.

The material used in this book from the above participation-observation process is collected in the *2013 Survey of Korean Chinese Living in Seoul* (2013SKCLS, Seoul Metropolitan City), the *2013 Survey on the Business of Garibong-dong* (2013SBG, my personal research), the *2008 Survey on the Korean Chinese Enclave* (2008SKCE, OKF), and the *2008 Factual Survey on the Satisfaction of Visiting and Employment System* (2008FSSVES, Ministry of Justice [MOJ] and Ministry of Labor [MOL]). The interview data includes 17 businessmen, four general workers, and one Korean. In addition to this, there are materials used from a book I published with my colleagues in 2012 with the support of the KCTN called *The South Korea We Met: The Oral History of Korean Chinese* (Seoul: Book Korea). Some of the materials collected for this book that are used here were not published in the final copy of that collection.[4]

Notes

1 See also Tsuda and Song (2019).
2 In this study the term "entrepreneur" refers not to those who invested a large amount of capital in South Korea and operated a company, nor to representatives of a Korean branch of a Chinese company, but to people who became entrepreneurs after immigration into South Korea.
3 See Cohen (1996), Soysal (1994), Bauböck (2006), and Castles and Davidson (2000) for further research of migration and citizenship.
4 The literature consulted includes (1) records of the activities of Korean Chinese groups collected through participant-observation processes and the records of local newspapers; (2) legal texts related to the change in legal status of Korean Chinese, government policies and press releases; (3) articles in academic journals, publications in academic journals, monographs, research service reports, local and public hearing documents; (4) articles in major domestic daily newspapers; and lastly, (5) government-produced reports including the "Statistical Yearbook of China", "Population and Housing Census" of Korea, "Statistical Yearbook of Immigration Statistics and Monthly Report (Ministry of Justice)", and the report on the "Status of Foreign Residents in Local Governments (Ministry of Government Administration and Home Affairs) (Seoul Metropolitan City)".

References

2008 Factual Survey on the Satisfaction of Visiting and Employment System (2008FSSVES). 2008. Ministry of Justice and Ministry of Labor.
2008 Survey on the Korean Chinese Enclave (2008SKCE). 2008. Overseas Korean Foundation.
2013 Survey of Korean Chinese Living in Seoul (2013SKCLS). 2013. Seoul Metropolitan City.
2013 Survey on the Business of Garibong-dong (2013SBG). Unpublished raw data.
Bauböck, Rainer, ed. 2006. *Migration and Citizenship: Legal Status, Rights and Political Participation*. Amsterdam: Amsterdam University Press.
Castles, Stephen and Alastair Davidson. 2000. *Citizenship and Migration: Globalization and the Politics of Belonging*. New York: Routledge.
Chang, Kyung-Sup. 2010. *South Korea under Compressed Modernity: Familial Political Economy in Transition*. London/New York: Routledge.
Chang, Kyung-Sup. 2012a. "Developmental Citizenship in Perspective: The South Korean Case and Beyond." pp. 182–202, in *Contested Citizenship in East Asia: Developmental Politics, National Unity, and Globalization*, edited by Chang, Kyung-Sup and Bryan S. Turner. London/New York: Routledge.
Chang, Kyung-Sup. 2012b. "Different Beds, One Dream? State-Society Relationships and Citizenship Regimes in East Asia." pp. 62–85, in *Contested Citizenship in East Asia: Developmental Politics, National Unity, and Globalization*, edited by Chang, Kyung-Sup and Bryan S. Turner. London/New York: Routledge.

Chang, Kyung-Sup. 2012c. "Predicaments of Neoliberalism in the Post-Developmental Liberal Context." pp. 70–91, in *Developmental Politics in Transition: The Neoliberal Era and Beyond*, edited by Chang, Kyung-Sup, Ben Fine and Linda Weiss. Basingstoke: Palgrave Macmillan.

Chang, Kyung-Sup. 2014. "Transformative Modernity and Citizenship Politics: The South Korean Aperture." pp. 163–180, in *South Korea in Transition: Politics and Culture of Citizenship*, edited by Chang Kyung-Sup. London/New York: Routledge.

Chang, Kyung-Sup and Bryan S. Turner. 2012. "Introduction: East Asia and Citizenship." pp. 1–12, in *Contested Citizenship in East Asia: Developmental Politics, National Unity, and Globalization*, edited by Chang, Kyung-Sup and Bryan S. Turner. London/New York: Routledge.

China Statistical Yearbook. 2010. Retrieved September 10, 2017. www.stats.gov.cn/tjsj/pcsj/rkpc/6rp/indexch.htm.

Cohen, Robin, ed. 1996. *The Sociology of Migration*. Cheltenham/Brookfield, VT: Edward Elgar.

Isin, Engin F. and Bryan S. Turner. 2007. "Investigating Citizenship: An Agenda for Citizenship Studies". *Citizenship Studies* 11(1): 5–17.

Jung, In-Sup. 1999. "Analysis of New Acts of Legal Status of Overseas Koreans" (in Korean). *Seoul International Law Journal* 6(2): 301–321.

Jung, Keun-Sik. 2013. "The Formation and Reconstruction of Korean Diaspora" (in Japanese). pp. 1–21, in *Transition of Intimate and Public in East Asia*, edited by Motoji, Mastuda and Keun-Sik Jung. Kyoto: Kyoto University Press.

Kim, Hyun-Mee. 2012. "The Emergence of the 'Multicultural Family' and Genderized Citizenship in South Korea." pp. 203–217, in *Contested Citizenship in East Asia: Developmental Politics, National Unity, and Globalization*, edited by Chang, Kyung-Sup and Bryan S. Turner. London/New York: Routledge.

Kim, Hyun-Mee. 2014. "The State and Migrant Women: Diverging Hopes in the Making of 'Multicultural Families'." pp. 147–159, in *South Korea in Transition: Politics and Culture of Citizenship*, edited by Chang, Kyung-Sup. London/New York: Routledge.

Kim, Jae-Eun. 2016. *Contested Embrace: Transborder Membership Politics in Twentieth-Century Korea*. Palo Alto, CA: Stanford University Press.

Ministry of Foreign Affairs. 1991. *Korean Diplomatic White Paper* (in Korean). Available at: https://www.mofa.go.kr/www/brd/m_4105/list.do?page=9&srchFr=&srchTo=&srchWord=&srchTp=&multi_itm_seq=0&itm_seq_1=0&itm_seq_2=0&company_cd=&company_nm= (Accessed: 21 Dec 2019).

Korean Immigration Service. 2008. *Korean Immigration Service Statistics (in Korean). 2008*. Seoul.

Korean Immigration Service. 2016. *Korean Immigration Service Statistics (in Korean). 2016*. Seoul.

Lee, Chul-Woo. 2012. "How Can You Say You're Korean? Law, Governmentality and National Membership in South Korea." *Citizenship Studies* 16(1): 85–102.

Lee, Hye-Kyung. 1994. "The Employment of Foreign Workers in Korea: Its Impacts on Labor Market." *Korean Journal of Sociology* 28(F): 89–113.

Lee, Hye-Kyung et al. 1998. *Korean Society and Foreign Workers* (in Korean). Seoul: Center for Future Human Resource Studies.

Lee, Jean-Young. 2002. "Issues and Implications: Korea's Policy towards the Ethnic Koreans Abroad" (in Korean). *Korea and World Politics* 18(4): 133–162.

Lee, Jong-Hoon. 2001. "Policy for Korean-Chinese and Right Directions of the Law for Overseas Koreans" (In Korean). *Studies of Koreans Abroad* 11(1): 165–190.

Light, Ivan H. 2005. "The Ethnic Economy." pp. 650–677, in *The Handbook of Economic Sociology* (2nd edition), edited by Smelser, Neil J. and Richard Swedberg. Princeton, NJ/Oxford: Princeton University Press; New York: Russell Sage Foundation.

Light, Ivan H. and Edna Bonacich. 1988. *Immigrant Entrepreneurs: Koreans in Los Angeles 1965–1982.* Berkeley/Los Angeles/London: University of California Press.

Light, Ivan H., and Steven J. Gold. 2000. *Ethnic Economy.* Bingley: Academic Press.

Light, Ivan H. and Stavros Karageorgis. 1994. "The Ethnic Economy." pp. 647–671, in *The Handbook of Economic sociology*, edited by Smelser, Neil J. and Richard Swedberg. Princeton, NJ: Princeton University Press; New York: Russell Sage Foundation.

Light, Ivan H., and Angel Sanchez. 1987. "Immigrant Entrepreneurs in 272 SMSAs". *Sociological Perspectives* 30(4): 373–399.

Loh, Yeong-Don. 1999. "A Study on the 'Act on the Immigration and Legal Status of Korean Nationals Residing Abroad" (in Korean). *Inchon Low Review* 2: 57–71.

Loh, Yeong-Don. 2002. "A Suggestion for the Amendments of the 'Law of Korean' Abroad" (in Korean). *The Korean Society of Journal International Law* 47(3): 97–119.

Marshall, Thomas Humphrey. 1950. *Citizenship and Social Class: And Other Essays.* London/New York: Cambridge University Press.

Park, Gi-Gap. 2001. "Legal Problems of Korean-Chinese in Korea" (in Korean). *Kangwon Law Review* 14: 301–323.

Park, Woo. 2012. "20 Years of Migration and Settlement of Korean Chinese in Korea: Between Compatriot and Foreign Worker" (in Korean), *New Migrant and Contents Plan for Korean Chinese* (conference paper), Overseas Korean Association, Seoul: Hankuk University of Foreign Studies.

Park, Woo. 2013. "Economic Incentives and Instrumental Nationalism: Focusing on the Korean Chinese in Korea" (in Japanese). pp. 289–306, in *Transition of Intimate and Public in East Asia*, edited by Motoji, Mastuda and Keun-Sik Jung. Kyoto: Kyoto University Press.

Park, Woo. 2017a. "Transnational Migration and Seoul's Korean Chinese" (in Korean). pp. 329–349, in *Sociology of Seoul: People, Space and Everyday Life*, edited by Seo, U-Seok, Mi-ree Byun, Baek-Yung Kim and Ji-young Kim, et al. Seoul: Nanam.

Park, Woo. 2017b. "Hierarchical Citizenship in Perspective: South Korea's Korean Chinese." *Development and Society* 46(3): 557–589.

Park, Woo. 2018. "Developmental State, Ethnic Minority, and Citizenship: Yanbian Koreans in Perspective." Paper Presented in the International Conference for *Developmental Citizenship(s) in China: Social Governance and Developmental Politics in Citizenship Perspective*, hosted by Korean Association of Comparative Sociology and Institute for China Studies of Seoul National University. 19 October 2018, Center for Asian Studies, Seoul National University.

Park, Woo. 2019. "The Asianization of Northeast China: Segmented Integration of Local Authority and Yanbian Korean Autonomous Prefecture." *Journal of Asian Sociology* 48(3): 377–413.

Park, Woo and Yong-Sun Kim et al. 2012. *The South Korea We Met: The Oral History of Korean Chinese* (in Korean). Seoul: Book Korea.

Seok, Hyun-Ho et al. 2003. *Workplace and Life of Foreign Workers* (in Korean). Seoul: Jisikmadang.

Seol, Dong-Hoon. 1999. *Migrant Workers and Korean Society* (in Korean). Seoul: Seoul National University Press.

Seol, Dong-Hoon. 2012. "The Citizenship of Foreign Workers in South Korea." *Citizenship Studies* 16(1): 119–133.

Seol, Dong-Hoon and John D. Skrentny. 2009. "Ethnic Return Migration and Hierarchical Nationhood: Korean-Chinese Foreign Workers in South Korea." *Ethnicities* 9(2): 147–174.

Soysal, Yasemin Nuhoglu. 1994. *Limits of Citizenship: Migrants and Postnational Membership in Europe*, Chicago, IL: University of Chicago Press.

Tsuda, Takeyuki and Chang-Zoo Song, eds. 2019. *Diasporic Returns to the Ethnic Homeland: The Korean Diaspora in Comparative Perspective*. London: Palgrave Macmillan.

Turner, Bryan S. 1986. *Citizenship and Capitalism: The Debate over Reformism*. London: Allen and Unwin.

Turner, Bryan S. 1990. "Outline of a Theory of Citizenship." *Sociology* 24(2): 189–217.

Turner, Bryan S. 1993. "Contemporary Problems in the Theory of Citizenship." pp. 1–18, in *Citizenship and Social Theory*, edited by Bryan S. Turner. London: SAGE.

Turner, Bryan S. 1997. "Citizenship Studies: A General Theory". *Citizenship Studies* 1(1): 5–18.

Turner, Bryan S. 2001. "The Erosion of Citizenship". *British Journal of Sociology* 1(1): 189–209.

Turner, Bryan S. and Kyung-Sup Chang. 2012. "Whither East Asian Citizenship?" pp. 243–254, in *Contested Citizenship in East Asia: Developmental Politics, National Unity, and Globalization*, edited by Chang, Kyung-Sup and Bryan S. Turner. London/New York: Routledge.

2 Legal status[1]

Korean Chinese as "Foreign Workers"

The logic of Foreign Worker policy and its problematic institutionalization

In the mid-1980s, labour shortage and rising wages for domestic workers prompted the South Korean government to set up an "Industrial Technical Training System" (ITTS) so that businesses could employ de facto Foreign Workers (Lim and Seol 2000a, 2000b). These workers were given the status of "Industrial Trainee" and began to receive official visas from the Ministry of Justice (MOJ) before entering Korea from 1991. Once these workers were integrated into the industrial field, the Ministry of Commerce and Industry (MCI) established rules to manage details like their contractual relationship with employers, extra benefits, and economic activities. However, before long, there were numerous cases of workers overstaying their visas or changing their place of work without official permission due to inexperience with Foreign Workers and the inefficient administration. This made the need for a dedicated agency clear and the government responded by assigning responsibility for the recruitment and introduction of Foreign Workers to the Korea Federation of Small and Medium Business (KFSMB) (MOJ 1993). The KFSMB set up the Industrial Technology Training Cooperation Team and established its own guidelines for the introduction and operation of "Industrial Trainee". Industrial Trainees first entered the country under these guidelines in May of 1994. In 1997 the KFSMB released their "Manuals for ITTS Employers" which set out procedures governing trainee recruitment, training period expiration and departure from the country. However, there were many problems despite these efforts at systematization: small and medium businesses complained about delays getting workers into the country and problems with workers suddenly disappearing without notice;

there were investigations of corruption in the system; and Nepalese workers bearing signs reading "We may be from a poor country ... but we have our basic human rights too" staged a sit-in protest in Myeong-dong Cathedral (Yamanaka 2010). These issues led to calls for fundamental improvements.[2]

In 1996, the Globalization Promotion Committee (GPC) set up the "Comprehensive Foreign Labor Policy". Under this policy, GPC decided to completely revise the ITTS rather than introducing the Employment Permit System (EPS) proposed by Ministry of Labor (MOL). However, because this proposed new system greatly altered the existing wage regulation-free arrangement, it immediately ran into opposition from other government departments recommending partial reform of the existing ITTS framework instead. These departments also argued that EPSs faced increasing labour burdens (*Hankyoreh* 1 August 1996a, 1996b).[3] This opposition stymied the GPC's original plan, and they had to settle for proposing a partial overhaul of the ITTS, which would be called the Training and Employment System (TES), to be put into action from 1998. Its main feature would be to allow some trainees to obtain an employment visa after their workmanship and related skills had been assessed (*Kyunghyang Shinmun* 10 September 1997). However, the Korea Employers' Federation (KEF) officially opposed this redesign as well (*Maeil Business News Korea* 24 September 1997), and the problem ended up being passed on to the next administration. The MOL also tried to amend the Immigration Control Act (ICA) for this introduction of TES, but the departments impacted made their opposition clear and claimed that the legislative amendment was difficult (*Hankyoreh* 24 October 1997). A compromise of sorts was finally reached, and the MOJ introduced the term "Trained Employee" into the ICA in December 1997 (over which they had control), along with details about trainee importation and management. On the 1st of April 1998, the E-8 Employment Training Visa was introduced alongside the C-4 (short-term employment), E-1 (for University Professors), and E-2 (Special Activities) visas in the Enforcement Decree of Immigration Control Act (Presidential Decree 1998, paragraph 1). From then on, after passing the Foreigner's Employment Training Qualification Exam and completing a two-year training period, Industrial Trainees were able to change their existing D-3 (training) visa to a Training Employment visa (E-8), which would provide a one-year guarantee of legal worker status.[4] On the 6th of February, 2000, the Small and Medium Business Administration (SMBA) announced that TES would be put into full-scale operation (KFSMB and KSBI 2001: 10–14, 2004: 46–53).

"Foreign Worker's" limited sphere of socio-economic activity

From the above we can see that foreigners receiving training in South Korean businesses were directly required by capital (especially small and medium size capital) and that they were imported into Korea through a "planned", state-led selection process. In this environment, Industrial Trainees faced various limits on their socio-economic activities. Not only was economic activity outside the workplace heavily restricted, but trainees were also not easily able to quit their job: any change of workplace or training plans had to be reported to the head of the relevant immigration office by the person or organization that invited the trainee to South Korea (MOJ 1991). From 1994, trainees had to receive a recommendation from the president of the KFSMB 60 days before visa expiration if they wanted to extend their stay (KFSMB 1994; MOL 1995),[5] and in 1996, it was decided that when trainees entered or left the country the head of their workplace had to immediately report this to the local immigration office. Moreover, once they entered the country the trainee's status (such as their place of work and training plans) was checked frequently (MOJ 1996). Under TES, trainees' status as labourers with the right to work might be recognized, but other rights and freedom were not granted (KFSMB and KSBI 2004: 46–57). From 2002, Industrial Trainees were supposed to stay at the same workplace and could only move if the employer did not want to keep the trainee on or if the business closed (Presidential Decree 2002, article 1 paragraph 5): changing workplace was rigorously restricted and controlled, and even when possible, it inevitably required them to go through a complicated bureaucratic process. As such, under the ITTS and TES, Foreign Workers were not truly incorporated into the labour market and could not engage freely in socio-economic activity. This groups' legal status in South Korea and the rights based on this legal status were prepared for the sake of the employer who decided to introduce them into the country, and according to the administrative agencies' economic logic. It was a logic secured by the state in law and policy, and employers who exploited the system's various problems and loopholes often made the trainees' situation worse.

Industrial Trainees' pay was based on South Korea's minimum wage system from the beginning of the policy (MCI 1992). The first three months, however, were considered a training period, and only 80% of the normal wage was paid during this time. Overtime work, night work, and holiday work was paid at a rate of 150% of the basic wage. And the trainees had to deposit 50% of their monthly wage into an instalment savings account at a bank predetermined by their country of origin. Korean Chinese trainees born in China, for example, had to use Industrial Bank.[6] These savings could not be withdrawn outside of exceptional circumstances such as the trainee's own death or illness, the bankruptcy of the training company, or a temporary suspension of operations at the company. Any other reasons would have to be approved by the president of the KFSMB (KFSMB 1997: 8–10).

At the time it seemed as if TES would make up for many of ITTS's limitations, and in terms of the transitional stages between ITTS and EPS it was a somewhat positive development. But TES severely limited the socio-economic activities of Foreign Workers. And because it tied the legal length of stay in South Korea to the training and employment period, this introduced a new risk for those with Foreign Worker status: if, when moving companies, a trainee's contract could not be finalized in time, they automatically became unregistered immigrants and lost the right to claim any kind of social security. Some employers took advantage of this situation to illegally exploit Foreign Workers.

ITTS, TES, and other policies relating to "Foreign Workers" were oriented towards industrial requirements. Under this system, Korean Chinese were not distinguished from other foreign labourers who were given the same rights.

Korean Chinese as the "Special Status of Overseas Korean"

The logic of Overseas Korean policy

From the formation of the South Korean government to the administration of Roh Tae-Woo and its "Nordpolitick" strategy, the purpose of South Korea's policy for Overseas Koreans can be seen as being shaped by regime competition with North Korea. The main object of this policy is the ethnically Korean residents and citizens (*hangukgyomin*) of liberal democracies in North America, Japan, and Europe (Oh 1983; Kim 1991), but in 1988, the *Special Declaration by President Rho Tae-Woo in the Interest of National Self- esteem, Unification and Prosperity* made clear that South Korea "will make necessary arrangement to ensure that Koreans residing overseas can freely visit both parts of Korea" and will "continue to seek improved relations with the Soviet Union, China and other socialist countries" (Diplomatic Chronology of Republic of Korea 1988: 538–540). In the *Follow-up*

Measures on the Implementation of the Open-door Policy for ensuring Free Visits of Overseas Koreans to South and North Korea, the government specified that "We will ensure that those Koreans residing in Communist-bloc countries can make free visits to the Republic of Korea" (DCROK 1988: 584). As a result of this policy change, ethnic Koreans from China and the Soviet Union could participate in the World Korean Athletic Meeting held in Seoul from September 26th to 30th, 1989. And with the opening of the Incheon-Shandong Intercity Passenger Ferry, it became easier for Korean Chinese to visit Korea to meet relatives (Ministry of Foreign Affairs 1990: 189–190). After the establishment of diplomatic ties between South Korea and China in 1992, Korean Chinese also began to enter Korea, not as "Overseas Koreans" but as Chinese citizens. These changes reflected South Korea's confidence that they had begun to secure economic superiority over North Korea.

The civilian government's (*moonminjeongbu*) so-called "new Overseas Korean policy" (*singyopojeongchaek*) was actually based on the existing policy (*gyominjeongchaek*). Its headline change was to extend the validity of the visitor's family visa issued to Overseas Korean, including Korean Chinese, from three months to two years – changes made to strengthen ties with the visitor's home countries (Ministry of Foreign Affairs 1996: 269). The government attempted to streamline the Overseas Korean policy in 1996 by clearly distinguishing between two categories: ethnic Koreans with South Korean nationality living abroad, who were dubbed "Overseas Korean nationals" (*jaeoegukmin*), and ethnic Koreans without South Korean nationality, who were called "Korean compatriots with foreign nationality" (*oegukjeokdongpo*). The former concept was applied to those receiving legal protection from the South Korean State. The latter was a much broader concept, concerning more general cultural and educational policies of the South Korean state (Ministry of Foreign Affairs 1997: 286–287). Regarding China's Korean Chinese as "Korean compatriots with foreign nationality", the South Korean government stated that

> despite the fact that, thanks to the Chinese government's policies protecting ethnic minorities, this group preserved Korean culture and language relatively well, we have to consider that compared to ethnic Koreans from other regions they have limited understanding of and sentiment towards their mother country (*mogukuisik*), and that the Chinese authorities are concerned about our government's excessive interest in them. So, to avoid impinging on

China's ethnic minority policy our policy should not be to offer direct governmental support, but to instead strengthen support from local private sector organizations and civil society.
(Ministry of Foreign Affairs 1997: 288)

The Overseas Koreans Foundation (OKF), established in 1997, is representative of the civilian government's systematic policy towards ethnic Koreans living abroad. In Osaka in November 1995 and in Los Angeles in September 1996, President Kim Young-Sam announced that the OKF centre would be established in Seoul and declared that he would be promoting wide-ranging project for Overseas Koreans (Ministry of Foreign Affairs 1997: 288–289). The Overseas Koreans Foundation Act (OKFA) of 1997 and the establishment of the OKF centre can be seen as an important milestone in the institutionalization and legalization of the South Korean government's relationship with Overseas Koreans. Through this system, ethnic Koreans from all over the world, including Korean Chinese living in China, began to be tied into a new official relationship with South Korea.

When President Kim Dae-Jung visited the United States in 1998 (while South Korea was reeling from effects of the 1997 Asian Financial Crisis), he asked Korean-Americans to help their mother country and promised to solve their issues with dual nationality. The MOJ subsequently began to properly examine the subject of immigration and residency status, including the problems with dual nationality, and the government proposed systematically revising the problematic legal status of Overseas Koreans (*Kyunghyang Shinmun* 26 August 26 1998). With this commitment, the 1999 Act on the Immigration and Legal Status of Overseas Korean (AILOK 1999) passed through congress with overwhelming support (154 votes in favour against only eight votes against and four abstentions) (Kim 2002: 87). So, within four years of the GPC establishing the category of Overseas Koreans (especially for the "Korean compatriots with foreign nationality"), the AILOK passed through congress and set in place the basic framework defining the legal status of this new category.

However, the AILOK made a distinction between populations of ethnic Koreans who left Korea after the formation of the Republic of Korea and those who continued living in China (*Korean Chinese*), the Soviet Union, or former Soviet Republics. The latter groups were omitted from the Overseas Koreans category. This discrimination did not pass unnoticed by the excluded groups, whose civil society groups, academics, and political circles all called attention to the problem. As a result, it was proposed in 2004 that the originally excluded groups be incorporated, and from 2007 the law was gradually applied to Korean Chinese (Park 2011).

Conditions and socio-economic right for the "Special Status of Overseas Korean"

Revision of the AILOK did not provide a stable legal status for all Overseas Koreans (including Korean Chinese). The state showed priority to Overseas Koreans in professional work. For example, anyone who had stayed in South Korea for six months or more as a professional, who had a master's or higher degree from a Korean university, or who had a professional job in their country of residence or third country could get the Special Status of Overseas Korean status, unless they had previously overstayed on a short-term visa (MOJ 2007a). The South Korean government started to expand the Special Status of Overseas Korean in 2009, making it available to a wider range of Overseas Koreans,[7] then also decided to grant the Special Status of Overseas Korean to people with specific roles in the secondary labour market (especially for the Korean Chinese workers).[8]

Those who received the Special Status of Overseas Korean began to be issued with Domestic Resident Registration Cards (*gugnaege-ososingojeung*). These ID cards had a big, positive effect on the holder's everyday life, especially for those who were used to the limitations associated with the "Alien Registration Cards" normally issued to non-citizens. Cell phone subscription, for example, was much easier, and the cardholders were eligible for the same contract conditions as full citizens. There were also other benefits extended to those with the Special Status of Overseas Koreans status. The maximum stay period was increased from two to three years (AILOK 2008a, article 10), and this could be extended even longer. Re-entry permits were also no longer necessary for those exiting and re-entering the country in the middle of their stay. Moreover, foreign nationals with the Special Status of Overseas Koreans were allowed to freely engage in employment or other economic activities in the primary labour market, as long as they were not damaging social order or economic stability (e.g. by violating customs law or regulation, or engaging in unskilled labour). Ethnic Koreans with foreign nationality who were registered residents in South Korea were also granted the same right to acquire, possess, use, and dispose of property as full citizens (except in military bases and facilities). They were permitted the same rights as full citizens to use domestic financial institutions and could receive the same interest rates (although capital transactions were still restricted in order to regulate against hot money).[9] Lastly, registered residents with the Special Status of Overseas Korean were eligible for health insurance after staying more than 90 days in Korea (AILOK 2008b, article 6-16).[10] However, people with the Special Status of Overseas Korean (Korean compatriots with foreign nationality) couldn't participate in elections or stand for office. They were, in sum, given economic rights but not political rights.

The selective relaxation of conditions for permanent residency and naturalization

Conditions for permanent residency

The South Korean government sought to achieve what they called an "orderly opening" by easing the requirements for permanent residency and improving the living conditions for residents. At first, they set the permanent residency income requirement for professional Foreign Workers at a level more than 4 times per capita income, assuring that only those with a higher economic status than ordinary Korean citizens were eligible. However, in 2007, the income requirement was reduced to a level corresponding to three times per capita income. They also altered the requirement so that Overseas Koreans with foreign nationality who had been residents in Korea in the past but were now living abroad were also eligible (MOJ 2007b).

After this the South Korean government granted the status of permanent residence to those who have lived over two years in the country with Overseas Korean status if they fulfil one of the following conditions: (1) have an annual income more than twice the per capita income for the previous year; (2) are over 60 years of age and receives a pension from overseas that is more than twice South Korea's per capita income; (3) have paid more than 500,000 KRW or more in property tax last year, or, despite not paying property tax themselves own (or lives with a family member who owns) a property with a considerable rent deposit; (4) have invested over 500,000 USD in South Korea; (5) are, or have been in the last three years, delegates for Overseas Korean organization, or corporate representatives recommended by the head of a foreign embassy (MOJ 2008, 2009a).

The government also relaxed the requirements for permanent residency eligibility for ethnic Koreans in the secondary labour market. However, rather than directly granting permanent residency in this case, candidates were able to apply once five years had passed since they first acquired resident status. This was thought of as a way to both help alleviate the shortage of skilled production workers and show gratitude to those who had worked diligently and obeyed domestic laws (MOJ 2007c). The policy at the time was actually to encourage worker circulation, so the amount of time workers could stay in Korea was actively limited. However, this meant that many workers had to leave Korea almost as soon as they managed to acquire some skill. That made it very difficult to form efficient employment relationships in the industrial field, an issue that negatively affected productivity levels.

Since 2009, the number of eligible candidates for permanent residency has been increasing quickly. This is particularly the case for Foreign Korean Workers in the secondary labour market, where conditions for permanent residency have been relaxed even more: workers with long service in certain areas of industry, people with the assets needed to cover living costs, and those with technical qualifications recognized by the South Korean government have all been added (MOJ 2009a). Those recognized as part of the wider Korean ethnic group have been able to apply for and receive the status of permanent resident much easier than other foreign citizens.

Conditions for naturalization

The naturalization process of foreign citizens normally takes one of five general paths:[11] general naturalization, simplified naturalization, special naturalization, naturalization through parents, and restoration of nationality. However, as the policy for the naturalization of ethnic Koreans was systematized, it became possible for ethnic Koreans, including Korean Chinese, to become South Korean nationals through a separate, additional process within the existing framework. This process was created in 2001 through the Established Rule of MOJ, No. 551.

In 2005, the Established Rule of MOJ, No. 729 further defined the concept of "Korean compatriots with foreign nationality" used for applications to acquire (or recover) nationality. This was defined as someone who had Korean nationality in the past or is the direct descendant of someone who did. Since Koreans in China who left the Korean peninsula (or its associated territories) before the foundation of the People's Republic of China on the 1st of October, 1949 or were born in China before that day were considered to have forfeited their Korean nationality, they wouldn't be included in this category. Those who thought they should be included and wanted to recover or acquire Korean nationality had to first prove that they or their forebears had been Korean citizens.[12] According to the 2005 ruling, this could be proved with a copy of your own family register; a copy of your mother's or father's family register along with a birth certificate proving your relationship to this family (notarized, or with an official document guaranteeing authenticity); a family register proving your relationship to a Korean citizen within four degrees of kinship (notarized, or with an official document guaranteeing authenticity); a genealogy with a letter of guarantee; and the results of genetic tests undertaken by an accredited medical institutions (MOJ 2005a). Since then, these standards have been changed somewhat, the most important change being the extension of four degrees of kinship to six in 2007 (MOJ 2007d) and to eight in 2013 (MOJ 2013).

Where an applicant could not prove that they themselves had been citizens of South Korea, it was possible to reacquire nationality by providing proof about to their parents. First of all, they would need a copy of the maternal grandfather's family register. Then they would need a family register proving one of their parent's is related to a Korean citizen within four degrees of kinship, and proof that this is actually their mother or father. Alternatively, they could provide a genealogy with a letter of guarantee, or the results of genetic tests undertaken by an accredited medical institution (MOJ 2005a).

These paths to naturalization were generally only open to those who had entered and stayed in South Korea legally. However, in rare cases, especially where there were "humanitarian" concerns, it was possible for ethnic Koreans living as undocumented immigrants to become naturalized South Korean nationals. According to the Established Rule of MOJ, No. 729 and No. 781 this was possible for: (1) those introduced into a South Korean family register (through marriage or adoption, for example) and their unmarried children; (2) the spouse and unmarried children of those who have received permission to reacquire South Korean nationality and have given up their previous nationality; (3) Ethnic Koreans with Chinese nationality (Korean Chinese) who entered South Korea legally before the resumption of diplomatic relations between China and South Korea on August 24th, 1992 (except undocumented immigrants and immigrants with fake passport) (MOJ 2005a, 2007e).

From 2013 a new system was introduced to allow the family of qualified applicants to stay in South Korea. Here, the concept of "family" extended to spouses, children, and the children's spouses. As such this rule could be applied to family members who were on the family register of the person possessing Korean nationality, or who were staying with them in South Korea. If a family member of a person who has reacquired South Korean nationality and given up (or has pledged to give up) their former nationality has entered the country illegally, but has an appropriate reason to stay in Korean (such as family reunification), then they could apply for permission to stay once the immigration rule violation had been dealt with. The only real exception was if they had been involved with people smuggling or passport forgery (MOJ 2013).[13]

At this point then, the eligibility criteria for South Korean nationality has been expanded to include not only Korean Chinese who used to have Korean nationality but Korean Chinese who cannot prove they used to be Korean national, Korean Chinese who have stayed in the country without permission of documentation, and even the families of Korean Chinese who have simply made an application for Korean nationality.

The status of "Overseas Korean with foreign nationality" – which has become almost equivalent to full Korean citizenship – has been granted selectively according to the individual's level of economic contribution. So Korean Chinese were not collectively acknowledged by the government as having the Special Status of Overseas Korean, and this was not a policy whereby all Korean Chinese could freely engage in economic activity within South Korea's labour market. It was a system that recognized only a certain class of Korean Chinese as the Special Status of Overseas Korean, and did so according to strict criteria. This included, first of all, Korean Chinese who possessed human and social capital that could be transferred to the primary labour market in Korea, or who possessed the economic capital to contribute to the expansion of private sector investment and/or help create employment in South Korea. Second, it included those who, in their role as professionals, or thanks to their association with particular parties, states, or organizations, could play an important role in the development of a positive, mutually beneficial relationship between South Korea and China. Third, Korean Chinese who were incorporated in the secondary labour market could also be granted the Special Status of Overseas Korean if they had shown that they could, and would, fill positions that were avoided, not only by South Korean workers but also by Foreign Workers.

Once gained the Special Status of Overseas Koreans granted rights effectively equal to full South Korean citizenship, meaning the range of socio-economic activity its holders enjoyed was very different to that of people with Foreign Worker status. For instance, the Domestic Resident Registration Card issued with the Special Status of Overseas Korean was comparable to South Korean citizen's Registration Card (*jumindeunglogjeung*), and because its holders could leave and re-enter the country without re-entry permits, it essentially allowed for permanent residency – the period of stay was not linked to employment contract like it was for Foreign Workers. Holders could also engage freely in economic activities outside the secondary labour market, buying and selling property just like South Korean citizens, and using domestic financial institutions just like full citizens as well. Health Insurance, too, was provided for those with the Special Status of Overseas Korean. The Special Status of Overseas Koreans even greatly improved holders' chances of being granted permanent residency of becoming a naturalized Korean as it opened up separate (and easier) tracks to permanent residency and naturalization unavailable to other non-nationals. So, although not all regulations pertaining to Korean Chinese with foreign nationalities could be removed, those incorporated into South Korea with the Special Status of Overseas Korean were legally and institutionally very different to other groups of Foreign Workers in secondary labour market.

It is clear that one portion of the criteria determining the Special Status of Overseas Korean eligibility according to the AILOK was an individual Korean Chinese's human and social capital, and another portion was the value of their long-term employment in one of Korea's unattractive jobs. The South Korean government displayed the nature of its blood-based nationalism in selecting ethnically Korean Chinese individuals to play the role of industrial worker (and investor) in South Korea's labour market. However, not all of the Korean Chinese population possessed the same human, social, and economic capital. And not all possessed the same skills. As such, those who could be incorporated into the primary labour market began to be systematically separated from those who could be included in the secondary labour market. This was the division between the "Special Status of Overseas Korean" and the "Foreign Korean Worker".

Korean Chinese as "Foreign Korean Worker"

From Employment and Management System (EMS) to Visiting and Employment System (VES) – the logic behind Overseas Korean labour force policy institutionalization

The EMS was introduced in 2002, when the AILOK's unconstitutional character had been acknowledged, and the collective action of Korean Chinese organization demanding that they be offered the same recognition offered to other groups of ethnic Koreans was in full swing.

EMS was designed to supplement the existing ITTS framework so that Overseas Koreans with foreign nationalities from countries such as China could be used in the service sector, manufacturing, construction, offshore fishing, and agricultural industries (Office for Government Policy Coordination 2002).

Under EMS, the South Korean government lowered the minimum age of Korean Chinese employees in Korea from 30 to 25 and allowed them to work in the construction industry. It also simplified the procedure for both job seekers and prospective employers (MOL 2004). With the lower entry age, the increased range of industries in which employment was possible, and the simplification of procedures for entry into the country and employment once there, it became much easier for Korean Chinese to enter South Korea and find employment.

However, from the 17th of August, 2004 EMS was absorbed into the 2003 EPS's procedures for "special" circumstances. The EPS was an early attempt at reducing the high rate of illegally employed Foreign Workers inadvertently caused by ITTS limitations. It was also supposed to improve the system's ability to adjust to changes in domestic economic and labour market conditions. To achieve these goals, it introduced a comprehensive legal system that prevented the employment of Foreign Workers without specific authorization and was calibrated to encourage the employment of foreigners in professional and technical fields (Song 1993: 88–91). It was hoped that EPS would alleviate the problems faced by Foreign Workers with Industrial Trainee status (such as human rights issues, and the ease with which they could fall into illegal employment or overstay their visa). Under EPS, when a company applied for the introduction of Foreign Workers, the government reviewed this application before granting the business owners with an employment permit and the Foreign Workers with a work permit. One significant feature was that Foreign Workers who received work permits in this way were guaranteed the same working conditions as domestic workers. However, these work permits were not easy to obtain, and with South Korean workers struggling to find domestic employment at the time, it was really a policy intended to minimize the impact of Foreign Workers in the domestic labour market (*Maeil Business News Korea* 14 February 1995a, 1995b).

Despite the EMS's limitations it was widely expected that the introduction of EPS would cause dispute among stakeholders. Regardless, a government-wide "Improvement Plan for the Policy of Foreign Laborer" was finalized in 2003 (OGPC 2002; MOL 2003). Meanwhile, after a cutthroat debate the National Assembly's Environment and Labor Committee passed the Foreign Laborer Employment Act (FLEA) on the 31st of July, 2003 (Environment and Labor Committee of National Assembly of ROK 2003). As a result, EPS was put into effect from August 17, 2004. Included in the EPS's "special" cases section were Korean Chinese who had already entered Korea with an F-1 (Korean relatives visiting) visa (Presidential Decree 2004, article 19).

In 2005, the MOJ began measures to introduce the VES to remedy the limitations of the existing EMS and EPS frameworks (MOJ 2007f: 1). This was not a simply about the introduction of Foreign Workers, but a policy regarding foreign ethnic Koreans (especially for the foreign Koreans workers from China and former Soviet Union) (MOJ 2005b). It looked to ease foreign ethnic Koreans into the South Korean workforce, a measure which was attractive given the worker shortage caused by the country's low fertility and aging. However, immigrants introduced in this way are absorbed into the low-income classes, and as such, it was necessary to consider the negative effect that this kind of immigration could provoke. This included the kind of human rights violations and social conflict that is brought about when immigration is mixed with a national identity that emphasized pure blood. The motivation for this policy was, then, not simply about solving workforce issues. There was a national consensus that human networks are important. The policy regarding ethnic Koreans from China and former Soviet Union countries could (1) strengthen the global ethnic Korean network, (2) develop the ethnic Korean society in China and former Soviet states, and (3) develop Korea's economy at a low cost (MOJ 2005b: 1).

The AILOK affected workers in the primary labour market but not those in the secondary market, where there was a labour shortage. To deal with this shortage the government decided to attract more Korean Chinese by expanding the AILOK to apply to overseas ethnic Koreans in both labour markets. This was achieved by combining the visitor visa and employment visa so that Korean Chinese visiting Korea were permitted to engage in employment without changing to an employment visa. This new visa, which was valid for four years and ten months and allowed stays of up to two years at once, permitted holders to engage freely in the secondary market (although participation in the sex industry or other occupations seen as immoral was restricted). Overseas Koreans without family (or relatives) in South Korea were allowed to work, but in order to prevent just anyone coming to work in the country by claiming Korean heritage, the Foreign Laborer Policy Committee (FLPC) established a visa quota and required applicants to provide Korean language test scores. Also, in order to prevent students from abandoning university education to find employment in South Korea, only Overseas Koreans over 25 years old were allowed to work. According to the MOJ, the long-term plan was to abolish the visa quota, allow absolute freedom to work in the country, grant the Special Status of Overseas Korean or resident status to all Overseas Koreans, and abolish the maximum stay period (MOJ 2005b: 6–12). As of 2017 Korean Chinese as Foreign Korean Worker can stay in Korea for a total of four years and ten months. If you are not employed at this point but still want to stay for the extra period, then you need to make a return trip to China.

When VES became the responsibility of the MOJ this policy began to undergo systematization (MOJ 2007f: 1). First, the MOJ eliminated various EMS restrictions. Once a business had been issued with an Overseas Korean Employment Certificate they could find and employ any Foreign Korean Worker without need for further authorization. Foreign Korean Workers could move freely between industries, and rather than applying for permission simply had to report the change to the relevant authority. Whereas under the previous EMS they were only permitted to work in 12 sectors (such as construction, manufacturing, fishing, and the service industry), they now had access to 32 sectors (MOJ 2006). This system was put into operation on the 4th of March, 2007.

In this way, VES brought together ITTS, TES, EMS, EPS, and the other policies covering industrial workforce and non-national ethnic Koreans. It was also a transition stage towards granting the Special Status of Overseas Koreans rights equivalent to those of full citizens. If Korean Chinese enter South Korea for the first time with the Special Status of Overseas Korean rather than Foreign Worker status then regulation governing their residency and economic activities dissolve. Through the visiting employment visa, the opportunities for Korean Chinese without relatives in the country to come to South Korea have increased as well as the period for which they can stay. For those who were already employed in Korea before VES was introduced, it became legal to find new employment through personal contacts rather than having to go through a government agency, as long as they reported the conclusion of their previous contract.

After the 2008 financial crisis, VES underwent some revision. From 2010, the FLPC limited the number of visiting employment visas to 330,000[14] and Korean Chinese entering South Korea began to be issued short-term multiple-entry (C-3) visas rather than visiting employment visas. Visiting employment status began to be granted only on successful completion of a course at a private technical training academy (which could be attended with a D-4 training visa). This is the policy as of 2017.

Socio-economic autonomy

In contrast to people with the "Special Status of Overseas Korean", who were prohibited from participating in most jobs in the secondary labour market, the status of "Foreign Korean Worker" was given to Korean Chinese who could be incorporated only into the secondary labour market.

Unlike under ITTS and TES, Foreign Korean Workers were now able to engage freely in economic activity in almost all areas of the secondary labour market. This is directly related to the fact that the labour market in Korea is constantly in need of industrial manpower. The Korean Chinese who were eligible for visiting employment were able to stay in Korea for up four years and ten months. During this stay, Korean Chinese were able to move freely in Korea's labour market. Importantly, unlike under previous systems, the employee-employer relationship was no longer skewed so far in favour of the employer. Their freedom was relatively well guaranteed. After staying in Korea for the maximum four years and ten months they could return to China and reapply for the same residency status as before. It was even possible to make the application in China, and then return to Korea with a short-term visa to wait for it to come through.

Although Korean Chinese living in Korea as a Foreign Korean Worker did not quite have equal status with Korean citizens, their socio-economic freedom within the labour market was similar. Moreover, if their skill in a specific industrial area increased enough, then it was possible for them to change their Foreign Korean Worker status to permanent residency, Special Status of Overseas Koreans, or even to acquire full nationality.

Summary

South Korea's Korean Chinese population began to migrate into the country from the second half of the 1980s. This was in response to the establishment of and amendments to Korea policies on foreign industrial manpower and Overseas Koreans. The state determined the hierarchical status (visa type) of these migrants based on their resources and capital. These were further differentiated, and Korean Chinese sought to upgrade their statuses to ones that offered more freedom. Being able to change their legal status was one of the reasons why the enclave entrepreneur class emerged and actively sought to leverage their class position to secure citizenship rights. Moreover, these policies allowed the population of the Korean Chinese enclave, which was an important market for the entrepreneurs, to remain in South Korea and have autonomy in the labour market. We can safely conclude that legal status was an important condition for the emergence of the enclave entrepreneurs.

Notes

1 This chapter has been published as Sections 2–5 of Hierarchical Citizenship in Perspective: South Korea's Korean Chinese, *Development and Society (Journal of Asian Sociology)* 46(3): 557–589.

2 The government decided that the issues with workers changing or abandoning their jobs without permission stemmed from low wages and suggested a minimum wage system. This would raise the basic monthly wage from 200–260 USD to 320 USD (260,000 KRW). The KFSMB also pushed for more comprehensive insurance for Industrial Trainees (who were at that point denied insurance against industrial accident), looking to increase the cap from 2 to 30 million won (*Maeil Business News Korea* 18 January 1995).

3 See this article for an analysis of the issues surrounding self-interest in the development of regulatory systems.

4 When the Industrial Trainee system began, trainees were given six months residency at most. From 1996, this was extended to two years.

5 Although, in practice, recommendations were not provided by the president himself but by those in more junior positions.

6 Workers from China, Bangladesh, and Thailand were assigned to Industrial Bank. Workers from Vietnam, the Philippines and Myanmar were allocated Kook-Min Bank. Workers from Uzbekistan, Pakistan, and Kazakhstan had to use Dong-Nam Bank, and Sri Lanka, Mongolian, and Nepalese workers were allotted Dae-Dong Bank.

7 Specifically, those who have been staying in South Korea for over six months while working in recruitment, cultural arts, trade management, or as professors; (2) graduates of four-year undergraduate programmes and students receiving scholarship from the South Korean government; (3) those with the right to permanent residency in Organisation for Economic Co-operation and Development (OECD) countries; (4) representatives and registered employees of corporations; (5) owners of private businesses with sales of more than USD 10,000 in the previous year; (6) multinational company executives, media executives and reporters, lawyers, accountants, doctors, artists, agricultural engineers, marine engineers, aviation engineers, researchers at research institutes, and university professors and associate professors at universities in their country of residence; (7) a delegate or deputy delegate of an officially recognized ethnic Korean associations for culture and art (officially recognized groups include the Joseonjok Entrepreneurs Association, the Korea International Trade Association, the Yanbian Korean Autonomous Artists Association, the Yanbian Korean Traditional Cuisine Association, and the Beijing Goguryeo Cultural Economy Study Group); (8) former and current members of the National Assembly, civil servants and employees of state-owned enterprises with more than five years of service;

(9) University professors (including associate professors and lecturers), principals of educational institutions for ethnic Koreans (also vice-principals, head teachers, and head secretaries), middle and high school teachers, elementary school teachers; (10) individuals who manage or want to manage small businesses (MOJ 2009b).

8 Specifically (1) people who have entered Korea with a short term or H-2 visa more than 10 times in the last two years (as long as they stayed less than 30 days each time), and those who stayed in the country less than 150 days in one year after entering with a visiting employment visa; (2) people with an H-2 visa who have graduated from a four-year undergraduate course and submitted a letter stating that they are not employed as an unskilled worker (MOJ, 2009b). In 2010, the South Korean government extended the Special Status of Overseas Korean to existing workers in the secondary labour market. This applied to (1) those who have worked for more than one year in the same position in manufacturing, agriculture, fishing, and care work, or as a household employee; (2) those who have worked for over six months in manufacturing, agriculture, or fishing and have acquired a work-related qualification while in Korea; (3) those who have stayed in the country for more than 200 days per year for the last two years, or those aged 63 or older. Korean Chinese workers in long-term employment within sectors with severe labour shortages can also qualify for the Special Status of Overseas Korean (MOJ 2010).

9 In this case, "hot money" refers to capital moved regularly and rapidly between financial markets to make use of different interest rates.

10 Refer to Jung (1999: 182–183) for additional explanation of the conditions applying to activity in the property and financial markets by residents with Overseas Korean status.

11 Lee (2012) has described various conditions of naturalization. Here I only focus on the conditions of naturalization for Korean Chinese.

12 See Kim's (2016) excellent research on the process by which *conceptual* compatriots became *legal* compatriots.

13 Providing all the supporting documents did not guarantee a successful application, however. There were cases when nationality would not be granted (e.g. if the applicant had lived or studied in North Korea, or if they had worked for the Communist Party, or in the military, or in government agencies). Where the documents were insufficient, exceptions could be made for individuals who had made important contributions to Korea's independence or were people of "national merit". These exceptions could also be made for their kin (MOJ 2005a).

14 At the same time, the number of people possessing Overseas Korean status increased, meaning that the total population of Korean Chinese in Korea could expand.

References

Act on the Immigration and Legal Status of Overseas Koreans (in Korean). 1999. Act No. 6015.

Act on the Immigration and Legal Status of Overseas Koreans (in Korean). 2008a. Act No. 8896.

Act on the Immigration and Legal Status of Overseas Koreans (in Korean). 2008b. Act No. 9140.

Environment and Labor Committee of National Assembly of ROK. 2003. *Act on the Employment of Foreign Workers* (in Korean). Seoul.

Hankyoreh. 1 August 1996a. "The Toughest TES" (in Korean). 3rd page.

Hankyoreh. 1 August 1996b. "Promote Foreign TES" (in Korean). 1st page.

Hankyoreh. 24 October 1997. "Foreign TES Postponed" (in Korean). 26th page.

Jung, Yeon-Soo. 1999. "A Review of Main Contents and Issue of 'Overseas Korean Act'" (in Korean). *Beobjo* 48(11): 178–193.

Kim, Bong-Seop. 2002. "The Background and Issues on the 'Overseas Korean Act'" (in Korean). *Gojoseondangunhak* 7: 75–134.

Kim, Heung-Soo. 1991. "Overseas Korean Policy of Korean Government" (in Korean). *Overseas Korean Policy Materials* 39: 73–79.

Kim, Jae-Eun. 2016. *Contested Embrace: Transborder Membership Politics in Twentieth-Century Korea*. Palo Alto, CA: Stanford University Press.

Korea Federation of Small and Medium Business and Korea Small Business Institute. 2001. *The Development Plan for Foreign ITTS* (in Korean). Seoul.

Korea Federation of Small and Medium Business and Korea Small Business Institute. 2004. *A Study on the Policy Efficiency of Foreign ITTS* (in Korean). Seoul.

Korea Federation of Small and Medium Business. 1994. *Operation Tips for Foreign ITTS Cooperation Projects* (in Korean). Seoul.

Korea Federation of Small and Medium Business. 1997. *Manuals for ITTS Employers* (in Korean). Seoul.

Kyunghyang Shinmun. 10 September 1997. "Introduction of Foreign ITTS" (in Korean). 2nd page.

Kyunghyang Shinmun. 26 August 1998. "Dual Nationality Virtually Acceptable – Half are Waiting in Anticipation, Half are Concerned about OILOK" (in Korean). 3rd page.

Lee, Chul-Woo. 2012. "How Can You Say You're Korean? Law, Governmentality and National Membership in South Korea." *Citizenship Studies* 16(1): 85–102.

Lim, Hyun-Jin and Dong-Hoon Seol. 2000a. *"An Introduction Plan for Foreign Worker's Employment Permit System"* (in Korean). Seoul: MOL Report.

Lim, Hyun-Jin and Dong-Hoon Seol. 2000b. "Foreign Labor Policy in Korea" (in Korean). *Korean Social Science Review* 22(3): 153–186.

Maeil Business News Korea. 14 February 1995a. "Government to Forestall Idea that Foreigners Should Be Paid Less" (in Korean). 38th page.

Maeil Business News Korea. 14 February 1995b. "Introduction of the Foreign EMS" (in Korean). 1st page.

Maeil Business News Korea. 18 January 1995. "How Is Foreign ITTS Changing? Foreign ITTS Will Be Implemented Soon and Discrimination Will be Corrected" (in Korean). 15th page.

Maeil Business News Korea. 24 September 1997. "Foreigners' Training Period Should Be Extended to 2 Years" (in Korean). 4th page.

MCI. 1992. *Management Guidelines for Foreign Trainees* (in Korean).

Ministry of Foreign Affairs. 1988. *Diplomatic Chronology of Republic of Korea* (in Korean). Seoul.

Ministry of Foreign Affairs. 1990. *Korean Diplomatic White Paper* (in Korean). Available at: https://www.mofa.go.kr/www/brd/m_4105/list.do?page=9&srchF r=&srchTo=&srchWord=&srchTp=&multi_itm_seq=0&itm_seq_1=0&itm_ seq_2=0&company_cd=&company_nm= (Accessed: 21 Dec 2019).

Ministry of Foreign Affairs. 1996. *Korean Diplomatic White Paper* (in Korean). Available at: https://www.mofa.go.kr/www/brd/m_4105/list.do?page=7&srch-Fr=&srchTo=&srchWord=&srchTp=&multi_itm_seq=0&itm_seq_1=0&itm_ seq_2=0&company_cd=&company_nm= (Accessed: 21 Dec 2019)

Ministry of Foreign affairs. 1997. Korean Diplomatic White Paper (in Korean). Available at: https://www.mofa.go.kr/www/brd/m_4105/list.do?page=7&srch-Fr=&srchTo=&srchWord=&srchTp=&multi_itm_seq=0&itm_seq_1=0&itm_ seq_2=0&company_cd=&company_nm= (Accessed: 3 Jan 2020).

MOJ. 1991. *Business Process Guidelines for Visa Issuance under ITTS* (in Korean). Directive No. 255.

MOJ. 1993. *Business Process Guidelines for Visa Issuance under ITTS* (in Korean). Directive No. 294.

MOJ. 1996. *Business Process Guidelines of Visa Issuance under ITTS* (in Korean). Directive No. 368.

MOJ. 2005a. *Business Process Guidelines for Reinstatement of Nationality for Compatriots with Foreign Nationality* (in Korean). Established Rule No. 729.

MOJ. 2005b. *Review of Policy Direction Regarding Overseas Korean with Foreign Nationality* (in Korean).

MOJ. 2006. *Expansion of the Scope of Employment Allowing Free Visits by Overseas Korean Compatriots* (in Korean).

MOJ. 2007a. *Restrictions on Immigration and Economic Activity Lifted for Professional Chinese and Former Soviet Compatriots* (in Korean).

MOJ. 2007b. *Residency Requirements Relaxed for Professional Foreign Workers, Overseas Koreans with Foreign Nationalities and Former Korean Chinese* (in Korean).

MOJ. 2007c. *Foreign Workers Can Also Acquire Permanent Residence: Ministry of Justice Establishes Standards to Recognize Importance of Skilled Production Workers* (in Korean).

MOJ. 2007d. *Business Process Guidelines for Reinstatement of Nationality for Compatriots with Foreign Nationality* (in Korean). Established Rule No. 785.

MOJ. 2007e. *Business Process Guidelines for Reinstatement of Nationality for Compatriots with Foreign Nationality* (in Korean). Established Rule No. 781.

MOJ. 2007f. *VES, an Engagement Policy towards Overseas Koreans with Foreign Nationalities* (in Korean).

MOJ. 2008. *Permanent Residency Acquisition Made Easier: Ministry of Justice Prepares to Relax Permanent Residency Requirements for Foreign Investors* (in Korean).

MOJ. 2009a. *Information on Additional Groups Being Eligible for Permanent Residency* (in Korean).

MOJ. 2009b. *Information on Chinese and CIS Compatriots Becoming Eligible for Special Overseas Korean Status* (in Korean).

MOJ. 2010. *Information on Employment Permits and Long-Term Residency for Compatriots Employed in Special Industries or with Visiting Employment Visas* (in Korean).

MOJ. 2013. *Business Process Guidelines for Reinstatement of Nationality for Compatriots with Foreign Nationality* (in Korean). Established Rule No. 1012.

MOL. 1995. *Guidelines for Protection and Control for Foreign Industrial Technical Trainees* (in Korean). Established Rule No. 258.

MOL. 2003. *Foreigner Employment Permit System for Sustainable Growth and Enterprise* (in Korean).

MOL. 2004. *Expanding Employment Opportunities for Compatriots with Foreign Nationalities* (in Korean). MOL.

Office for Government Policy Coordination. 2002. *Improvement Plan for the Policy on Foreign Laborers* (in Korean).

Oh, Chae-Gi. 1983. Government Put Emphasis on Social Stability and Settlement of Overseas Korean" (in Korean). *Overseas Korean* 9: 8–9.

Park, Woo. 2011. "A Study on the Transition of Korean Chinese 'Organization' and Struggle for Recognition in Korea" (in Korean). *Economy and Society* 19: 239–265.

Presidential Decree. 1998. *Enforcement Decree of Immigration Control Act* (in Korean). No. 15764.

Presidential Decree. 2002. *Enforcement Decree of Immigration Control Act* (in Korean). No. 17579.

Presidential Decree. 2004. *Enforcement Decree of Act on the Employment, ETC, of Foreign Workers* (in Korean). No. 18314.

Song, Byung-Joon. 1993. *Improvement Plan of Industrial Labor Force: Focus on Foreign Labor Force* (in Korean). Seoul: Korea Institute for Industrial Economics.

Yamanaka, Keiko. 2010. "Civil Society and Social Movements for Immigrant Rights in Japan and South Korea." *Korean Observer* 41(4): 615–647.

3　Enclave

The enclave as a historical theatre

Until the 1960s, Guro-dong ("dong" meaning administrative district of "gu"), where the Korean Chinese enclave is now located, was a quiet, rural area far from the centre of Seoul. It was mostly fields and rice paddies, but there were 5,442 houses, which accommodated about 28,000 people. A U.S. ammunition depot was located in the mountains, and there was a small camp population by people displaced by the redevelopment of downtown Seoul. All this changed in 1964 when the Export Industry Complex Promotion Committee decided to establish the Korea Export Industrial Complex in Guro-dong. The industrial estates were constructed according to a series of plans "to enable corporation who were to move into the industrial complex begin production activities through the lease and sale of buildings and land that had been built and created by the government." They were not just factory after factory – they included service facilities or communal facilities for railways, roads, power, water, and other production activities (Korea Export Industry Corporation 1994: 169–171). The construction of the first industrial complex in Guro-dong was completed in late 1966. Two years later, a second complex was completed to the west of the first. This was followed by a third, completed in 1973, which lay a little further west.

The park was established to help set up an export industry. The idea was to introduce technology and products via the Korean-Japanese entrepreneurs, but this group did not invest as much as expected after the first complex was completed. So, when the second zone was finished, the government set aside some space to attract big corporations. Restrictions that prevented companies from selling products domestically were dropped immediately after the complex's completion. Regulations on export duties were relaxed from the end of the 1970s, and small-scale urban domestic companies continued to move into the Guro Industrial Complex (GIC).

The GIC was created in accordance with the national policy goal of export-oriented industrialization, and evolved to meet the industrial demands of Seoul and the metropolitan area (Lee 2012). Strategic changes to the policy of state-centred export and development prompted and promoted urbanization in southwest Seoul. The industrial complex, located at the intersection of the Gyeongin and Gyeongbu rail lines, became a link between Seoul, its metropolitan area, and the residential area of the complex's labour force. In 1990 "The Guro Modernization Plan" enlarged the service industries in the complex's fringes (Son 2012), and the area also came to provide housing for those working in the local manufacturing and service industries.

By this time the GIC had also become a key locale in modern Korean history. Hagen Koo (2002: 23) even argues that it was here where a working class first formed in Korea. The Guro Strike of 1985, for instance, was the most important labour struggle of the early 1980s. This event was closely linked to the political struggle for democratization that was made during the country's industrialization process, and was a major turning point in the Korean labour movement – a precursor to the coming working-class movement (Koo 2002: 184–186).

With the establishment of the industrial complex, the concentration of the labour force, and the urbanization of Seoul that accompanied industrialization, Seoul authorities felt the need to establish administrative districts. The Guro area, which belonged to Yeongdeungpo-gu, became Guro-gu in 1980. This new district was composed of Guro-dong, Garibong-dong, Siheung-dong, Doksan-dong, Gocheok-dong, Gobong-dong, Yudong, Kudong, Onsudong, Cheonwangdong, Hangdong, and Shindorim-dong (Seoul Guro-gu 1997: 29–30). Industrial Complex No. 1 was incorporated into Guro-gu and later called "Guro Digital Complex". In 1973 Gwanak, which had been part of Yeongdeungpo-gu from 1963, became an autonomous district. It lies adjacent to GIC, Chowon-dong, Sinsa-dong, and Minseong-dong (Seoul Gwanak-gu, 1996: 55–57). Later, Geumcheon-gu was formed in 1995 when Siheung-dong, Gasan-dong, and Doksan-dong separated from Guro-gu. The second and third complexes are located in Gasan-dong (Seoul Geumcheon-gu 1997: 36–37). At their centre is an area called "Gasan Digital Complex". As such, the industrial park, which was originally built in the Guro area of Yeongdeungpo-gu, now neighbors Yeongdeungpo-gu, Guro-gu, Gwanak-gu, and Geumcheon-gu.

It, along with the housing for its workers, came to be "shared" by four autonomous regions.

Industrialization, democratization (labour movements), urbanization, and the neo-liberalization of South Korea are visible in the historical theatre of the Korean Chinese enclave.

Settlement

As mentioned in the previous chapters, since the establishment of diplomatic relationship between Korea and China, many Koreans began move to South Korea, and most of them were in the lower economic classes of Korean society in China. Table 3.1 shows the former socio-economic status of Korean Chinese labourers while in China. A look at average age by period of entry, and average monthly wage for their job in China reveals that their salaries in the South Korea were about 6.6 times higher. Considering absolute figures in isolation, average monthly wage seems high compared to Chinese averages, but the figures seems relatively low if "age at time of entry" is combined with "salary adjusted (increased) according to work experience". Between 2004 and 2008, for example, the average age of Korean Chinese entering Korea was between 44 and 47, and their monthly salary in China had been approximately 1,200 to 1,400 yuan. While their salaries increased slightly over a four-year period, this increase owed to yuan appreciation, so there was no increase in absolute value over their Chinese salaries (see Table 3.1).

Table 3.2 shows the outcome of determinants on the expected stay duration of Korean Chinese workers. Model 1 shows that the individual's sex, age, and educational background do not significantly impact the expected stay duration. When the socio-economic situation in China is considered, we see that the wider the gap in salary (the lower the salary in China) the longer the expected stay in Korea. Those who borrowed money from acquaintances or financial institutions rather than using their own funds also wished to stay for a long period. This was also true the more times the worker had exited the country and returned. As for variables affecting socio-economic situation in Korea, individual attributes again had no impact, however, the workers' situation in China did have an impact. The higher their wages in Korea, the greater amount remitted to China each month, and the greater their satisfaction with their present job, the longer the worker wanted to stay (Park 2013: 172).

As of 2016, there are 48,954 Korean Chinese in Yeongdeungpo-gu, 41,098 in Guro-gu, 25,331 in Geumcheon-gu, and 20,991 in Gwanak-gu.

Table 3.1 Monthly salary by job type, average age at time of entry, former job in China (Units: x's, yuan (RMB), age)

		Unemployed	Agriculture	Self-employment	Public Service	Professional	Worker	Other	Total
2008	Wage gap	6.5	8.0	5.1	4.5	5.5	6.5	5.9	6.2
	Chinese salary	1,300	1,048	1,744	1,706	1,757	1,359	1,475	1,414
	Avg. age	50	51	47	49	46	43	46	47
2007	Wage gap	7.4	7.4	5.1	5.3	5.3	6.4	5.3	6.3
	Chinese salary	1,366	1,254	1,757	1,702	1,775	1,420	1,763	1,463
	Avg. age	40	48	46	46	43	47	40	46
2005–2006	Wage gap	9.4	8.3	5.7	6.4	5.1	7.2	6.9	6.9
	Chinese salary	1,000	1,110	1,594	1,810	2,033	1,244	1,280	1,344
	Avg. age	42	46	43	48	35	48	47	45
Before 2004	Wage gap	8.1	8.5	6.2	5.7	5.3	7.0	7.2	7.1
	Chinese salary	1,208	1,062	1,476	1,808	1,835	1,289	1,262	1,298
	Avg. age	37	47	43	48	39	43	41	44
Total	Wage gap	7.7	8.0	5.5	5.5	5.3	6.7	6.3	6.6
	Avg. age	1,238	1,128	1,641	1,757	1,835	1,337	1,443	1,387

Source: 2008 Factual Survey on the Satisfaction of Visiting and Employment System.

Note: Chinese salary was estimated by job type, based on salary earned in Korea in addition to exchange rate and average wage differential at the time of survey.

Table 3.2 Determinants of expected stay duration of Korean Chinese workers

	Model 1 (N = 952) beta	Model 2 (N = 863) beta	Model 3 (N = 658) beta
Sex	−.008	−.005	.046
Age	−.044	−.054	−.052
Education	.008	.020	−.005
Salary comparison		.124***	.107**
Entry cost path		−.072*	−.085*
No. of times entered		.092**	.090*
Total cost of immigration		−.030	−.002
Avg. monthly wage			.101*
Avg. working hrs./day			.061
Avg. monthly savings			.044
Ave. monthly remittances to China			.095*
Length of stay (as of present)			.036
Family, relatives, and friends			.070
Job satisfaction			.184***
Constant	75.624***	53.922***	88.771***
R Square	.002	.131	.276

Source: 2008 Factual Survey on the Satisfaction of Visiting and Employment System.

Notes: Salary comparison denotes the differential between Korean salary and Chinese salary calculated by exchange rate at the time of survey. Entry cost path (variable): 1 = worker used his/her own personal assets, 0 = worker borrowed funds from an acquaintance or through financial institutions. Family, relatives, and friends (variable): 1 = information or help received when there came mostly from family members, 0 = all other cases. Job satisfaction: average value figured using a three-point scale for "salary level", "working hours", "content of work", "work environment", "living environment", "relationships with Korean citizen colleagues", "relationship with Korean citizen boss", and so on.
* $p < .05$.
** $p < .01$.
*** $p < .001$.

The percentage of foreign residents in Guru-gu increased from 6.4% in 2008 to 10.1% in 2015. Over the same period, it increased from 8.9% to 13.3% in Yeongdeungpo-gu, from 7.3% to 11.0% in Gumcheon-gu and from 2.6% to 5.2% in Gwanak-gu (Ministry of Public Administration and Security 2008, 2016). So most of the population in the area we are looking are South Korean nationals, but around 10% have foreign nationality.

In terms of absolute numbers, Yeongdeungpo-gu Daelim 2-dong has the largest number of Korean Chinese residents at 8,373, followed by Guro-gu Guro 2-dong with 7,475. There are 6,561 in Guro-gu Garibong-dong, 4,473 in Guro 4-dong, 4,359 in Geumcheon-gu Doksan 3-dong, and 3,993 in Yeongdeungpo-gu's Daelim 3-dong. This is followed by 3,392 in Gumcheon-gu's Gasan-dong, 3,041 in Daelim 1-dong in Yeongdeungpo-gu, and 3,028 in Guro 5-dong, Guro-gu (as of the first quarter of 2016, Ministry of Justice immigration policy headquarters). If we consider that Guro Complex No. 1 is located in Guro-gu's Guro 3-dong, and that complex Nos. 2 and 3 are in Gumcheon-gu's Gasan-dong, we can see that area where Korean Chinese and other non-South Koreans are concentrated is spread across the four administrative regions surrounding the GIC. The first concentration of Korean Chinese residents was formed in the Doksan-dong, Garibong-dong, and Guro-dong areas. As these area became saturated, new entrants expanded to neighbouring areas such as Daelim-dong.

Once they had fulfilled the functional conditions made by the state, Korean Chinese began to become naturalized South Korean citizens, acquire permanent residence, or change their status to those such as Overseas Korean that provide strong economic rights. These changes to legal status have ensured their residence, and since economic opportunities have continued to present themselves, their stay in Korea has changed from temporary to permanent.

If we compare the initial (at point of entry) and present legal statuses of the 423 Korean Chinese migrants we have data for, we find that 19.9% now have South Korean nationality, compared to 1.2% who arrived with it. Permanent residence, which only 1.2% enjoyed when they first arrived, is now held by 9.9%, and possession of Overseas Korean Status has risen from 12.7% to 42.6%. Marriage visas are also now held by slightly more of our sample (2.8%, as compared to 1.5% initially). Other statuses have seen a fall: At present 19.3% have a visiting employment visa – and this was the status 27.7% of the sample entered the country with. The fall is even sharper for foreign student visas, with only 2.4% having this status now, compared to 16.5% originally. Only 5.6% hold a different status from those already mentioned (down from 39.2%). These people sought to acquire citizenship or statuses equivalent to citizenship (permanent residence or Overseas Korean status) by going through a series of status changes. Some may have only needed to change status once, but others will have had to go through the process as many as five times. When interviewed, 342 (out of 425) were actually in the process of changing their status or were planning to do this in the future. 19.9% were seeking citizenship, 52.6% permanent residence, 17.0% Overseas Korean status, 5.3% a visiting employment visa, and 5.3% were looking for other, short-term visas (2013SKCLS).

These people had spent varying amounts of time in South Korea – the longest was 21 years, the shortest just one year. To put this into perspective, as the survey was conducted in 2013, 21 years in South Korea means the former participant had been in the country since 1992, the year when China and South Korea restored diplomatic relations. The length of time participants had lived in the enclave ranged from one to sixteen years. Most of the respondents had come to South Korea because of the visiting employment system that began operating from 2007. Some began living the enclave immediately after arriving from China, others had lived in other parts of Korea first (2013SKCLS).

A stable legal status in the country also influenced the family formation of Korean Chinese. Most of the early migration to South Korea was individual. We can determine this from the fact that there are relatively many women in the low-age groups and relatively few in the higher age groups. This suggests that many migrants came on their own rather than with families or a spouse (Park 2015; Park et al. 2015). Furthermore, the "transnational familyization" of the Korean Chinese population (Park 2006) was also the result of early individual migration.

However, as policy changed, family composition also changed. The proportion of Korean Chinese who have children in the enclave (301 cases) with one child in South Korea was 37.8%, 9.5% had two children 9.5%, and 1.5% had three children in South Korea. 51.2% didn't have children in South Korea, but did have children who lived in China or another country. About half of the respondents with children were living with at least one of their children in South Korea. Looking at the total number of children the respondents had, and the number of children who were living in South Korea with the respondents we can see that 40.2% of people with one child, lived with that child in South Korea. Seventy-one of the participants had two children, and of these, 25.4% lived with both in South Korea and 33.8% lived with one. Only six people had three children, of these people, 16.7% had one of these children living with them in South Korea, 16.7% had two children in the country, and 50.0% lived with all three together in South Korea. It seems that many of the respondents with children lived with them all together in South Korea (2013SKCLS).

We also looked at where the children and spouses lived. 14.9% of two-person households all lived together in South Korea. This was the case for 7.7% of three-person households, and 1.5% of four-person households. In total 24.1% of the respondents had their entire family living in South Korea. Many had family dispersed across South Korea and China (49.9%), and a handful (2.4%) had family in South Korea and another, third, country. A few (3.1%) had family in South Korea, China and a third country too. This means their family was dispersed across three states. Although Korean Chinese families display a transnational character, but they were also reuniting in Korea. Furthermore, the 20.6% who are unmarried may find a partner in Korea and start a family, meaning the number of the family members living in Korea will constantly shift (2013SKCLS).

It is also possible to deduce the tendency of the family unit to settle down through the changes in the children's educational institution (81 cases). 45.7%, of families had children in day care and kindergarten. 43.2% had children in elementary school, 12.3% had children in middle school, and 2.5% had children in high school. 80.2% of these children started their education with childcare centres or kindergartens in South Korea. 8.6% of children were educated in Korea from elementary school level, and 6.2% from junior high school level. Some students were enrolled in Korean universities and graduate schools, but most of these had graduated Chinese high schools or universities before studying in Korea (2013SKCLS).[1]

The number of children attending Daerim-dong's D elementary school whose parents have a transnational marriage or are foreign citizens is steadily increasing. As of April 2014, this was the background of 35% (182) of the school's 518 students. This percentage increased in the lower grades, reaching 55% in the first and second grades. Among the students whose parents were foreign nationals there those whose family were all Korean Chinese – this was the case for 20 in the first grade, 11 in the second, 22 in the third grade, 21 in the fourth grade and six in the sixth grade. If we were to include Korean Chinese families who had acquired South Korean citizenship, the number of children would be greater (Cho 2015: 20).

As the population of the settlement increased and the composition of the families altered, the type of housing also changed. 14.6% were living in the basement (*banjiha*) of small apartment buildings and 60.8% were living in the higher levels (including the rooftop apartments) of these buildings. 7.6% lived in tall apartment buildings and 5.1% lived in their own store. A further 3.5% lived in shared residences (*gosiwon*), dormitories, or shelters (*swimteo*). Those who lived in dormitories were often provided this accommodation by their company. The shelters were accommodation provided by Korean Chinese organizations or churches to people having difficulty finding a place to live. 1.4% lived in "Officetels" – studio apartments in semi-commercial buildings. 0.8% resided in houses. 6.2% lived in other kinds of accommodation, such as that provided to workers by employers or for live-in carers. In the enclave, Korean Chinese residents paid an average deposit of 7.52 million won for rented apartment, and an average monthly rent of 0.39 million won (*wolsei*). To lease an apartment rent free required an average deposit of 47,166,600 won (*jeonsei*) (2013SKCLS).

The market

The enclave was an area of economic production. Of the Korean Chinese residents, service workers were overwhelmingly the majority, at 86.8%. 4.4% worked in manufacturing, 3.2% in construction, and 5.6% in other sectors. These people were part of the concentrated local labour market, earning an average monthly salary of 1.82 million won, working an average of 10.5 hours a day and resting on average 6.4 days a month. They secured employed through various networks. 32.2% of the respondents found work through advertisements placed in local newspapers or magazines. 16.7% found out about their job from internet, 10.3% found work through intermediary agencies such as employment centres, and 10.2% found out about their job through family members or friends (2013SKCLS).

Free newspapers in the enclave mainly informed the locals about immigration policies and policies related to Overseas Koreans and covered the daily life of the local residents. They also posted jobs and employment information. Influential local newspapers include CKTN and Dongpo World Newspaper. Employment agencies provided employers with quick and easy access to job seekers. If an employer needs to hire someone urgently, or if the job conditions are particularly favourable, advertisements may be posted on the door or window of an employment agency. In addition to the type of business, salary, bonus, gender, age, working area, and the availability of accommodation, the listings provide information about visa conditions and possibilities. This informs potential employees about the visa status of current employees and whether or not employees with long service at the company can obtain the Overseas Korean Status (referred to on the listing as "F4") (see Table 3.3).

Korean Chinese from other regions visited the area due to this wealth of employment information. Mrs C (54 years old) lived in

Table 3.3 Advertisement of employment agency in Daelim 1-dong (24 April 2014)

Type of Business	Visa	Monthly Salary (Million Won)	Bonus (%)	Sex	Age	Region	Room and Board
Automobile components production	F-4 Changeable	1.7~2.0	30		Under 40	Asan	
Assembling electric components		Over 1.5				Hwaseong	Provide
Ulsan Hyundai dockyard[a]	H-2	Over 2.4		M	20~49	Ulsan	
Duct production[a]		Over 1.9				Gwangju	Provide
Dish case production[a]		Over 2.0					Provide
Sun roof production	Changeable	1.7~2.0					Provide
Electronics company (two Shift)	F-4, F-5, F- 6	2.65	40	All	36~42		Provide
Motel cleaning		Over 1.7		All		Metropolitan Area	Provide
Plastic sash production	Changeable	Over 1.7		All			Provide
Laver production[a]		Over 2.0		All		Haenam	Provide
Automobile components		170~200	30~40	All	Under 50	Hwaseong	
Plastic house cultivation[a]				F			Provide
Cell phone components production[a]		Over 2.0					Commute
Automobile components production	F-4 changeable	1.7~2.0	300		Under 40	Asan	

Job	Pay	Sex	Age	City	Housing
Simply assembling cell phone[a]	2.0~2.65	F			
Restaurant kitchen assistant	1.7~1.8	F	Under 58	Seoul	Commute
Restaurant hall service[a]	170	F	45	Seoul	Commute
Beefarm[a]	150	M		Jeonju	Provide
Restaurant kitchen assistant[a]	5~6 thousand won per hour	M		Seoul	Commute
Motel cleaning and management[a]	300	Couple		Uijungbu	Provide
Eel restaurant hall service[a]	180				Provide
Fish sales[a]	220	M	Under 50		Provide
Motel cleaning[a]	160	F	Under 57		Provide
Eel farm[a]	160	M	60		Provide
Construction odd-job worker[a]	70 thousand won per day	M			
Waste classification[a]	160	M	Under 65		Provide
Ox bone soup restaurant[a]	320	Couple	Under 57		Provide
Construction odd-job worker[a]	70 thousand won per day	M	Under 50		
Office[a]		All	Under 35	Seoul	
Housekeeper	150	F	Under 60		Provide

Note
a "Urgent Need".

Anyang but was inquiring about day care or nanny jobs at the job centre in Daelim 1-dong:

> There are a lot of Gyopo [ethnic Koreans born outside Korea] living in this area, so there are a lot more employment agencies and lots of jobs advertised in them. I had some spare time so I came here specifically to find a job. I ask friends and acquaintances, of course, but I often come to these employment agencies.
>
> (Mrs C, Female, 54)

A stream of workers commuted flowed in and out of the enclave. Female workers employed by small-and medium-sized manufacturing companies commuted in on public transport. Non-regular, temporary, or one-day workers came only when work called, rather than coming in regularly (Park et al. 2015).

The enclave was also an area of consumption. People from the same province or university held gatherings, alumni gathering, and enjoyed the taste of home offered in the enclave's restaurants (see Table 3.4).

The enclave also provided Korean Chinese with legal and administrative services. As Korean Chinese workers were integrated into the Korea's secondary labour market, lawyers specializing in employment, regulation, and documentation appeared. They consulted on and solved a variety of issues in the labour market, including employment contracts, retirement, turnover, industrial accidents, and wages. Services provided by the regulatory lawyers (*nomusa, haengjeongsa, beobmusa*, etc.) included complaints, complaints, petitions, administrative judgements, notarization and certification, extensions of stay, invitations and adoption, tax consultation, genetic testing, and divorce counselling. They also helped people apply for nationality changes and with registering permanent residences.

Table 3.4 Number of customers of restaurant in enclave (Units: Person, %)

	Less than 10	*10~20*	*20~30*	*30~50*	*50~100*	*More than 100*	*Total*
Weekday	20.7	36.4	22.3	10.9	8.2	1.6	100.0 (N = 184)
Weekend	9.2	19.0	30.4	17.4	15.8	8.2	100.0 (N = 184)

Source: 2013 Survey of Korean Chinese Living in Seoul.

Travel agencies in the enclave also acted as immigration and administrative agencies as well as more usual services such as domestic travel and holidays to Southeast Asia. C Travel Agency in Daerim 2-dong said that it provides a number of services related to the legal status of Korean Chinese in South Korea. These included: "Changing C-3 visas to H-2 visas" and "Changing C-3-2 visas to F-4 visas". They could assist customers with applying for permanent residency or Korean nationality after they had stayed for five years in the country. They claimed that any visa could be changed to an F-4 visa, and that invitation visa could be issued with a 100% success rate for children less than 25 years old. They also offered to help obtain 90-day tourist visas, even for Han Chinese customers.

The company also provided services for Chinese businesses, such as issuing and notarizing Chinese criminal record check certificates, and issuing new Chinese ID cards. These services brought people into the enclave. Mr Y (65), for example, who lived in Incheon, explained that he came to because,

> My H-2 is expiring soon so I have to go back to China. I came to get advice on when I can come back here, how I can come back here, and, if possible, to apply for a visa and buy a plane ticket.
>
> (Mr Y, male, 65)

In order for Korean Chinese to change their residence status in Korea, they had to complete a course at a private educational institute (academy) and then obtain a certificate to show that they are a skilled labourer. Certified academies appeared in the dwelling place from the year 2012 to help meet the resulting demand. Not all of the students enrolled in these academies lived in the area. For example, K(1), a male aged 33 who lived in Jongro said,

> I came to Korea on a C-3, visa, changed it to D-4, then changed it again to a H-2. Now I want to change it to an F-4 visa I have to attend an academy. I am trying to get a gardening certificate.

In another instance K(2), a female aged 31 who lived outside of Seoul, in Uijeongbu, said, "I am going to get a baking certificate so that I can change my visa".

Furthermore, there are agencies that offer comprehensive counselling services, such as the Construction Workers Support Center, which is run by the Construction Workers Mutual Aid Association. This provides construction workers with counselling services for on hot to quit smoking, health check-ups and consultation on problems like delayed wages, industrial accidents and unfair dismissal. There are also institutions operated by the local government office, such as the Guro-gu Workers' Welfare Center.

Since the late 1980s, industrial labour policies and the Overseas Koreans' policy have defined the Korean Chinese ethnic group as "Foreign Workers", "Overseas Koreans", or "Korean Foreign Workers". This structure changed according to policy. Whereas in the early days of migration, most of the Korean Chinese population were categorized as Foreign Industrial Manpower, later the population mostly came to be classified as Korean Foreign Workers or Overseas Koreans. This change meant that the number of people who could be legally employed and could choose how and where to live increased. The changes in visa regulation and laws encouraged family migration rather than individual migration, and many of the enclave's Korean Chinese lived in South Korea with their whole family. This helps to explain the trends we see in the way Korean Chinese have settled in Korea. Their enthusiasm for enrolling their children, whether they were born in China or Korea, into educational institutions in Korea, is also significant here. Moreover, legal statuses granting socio-economic autonomy guaranteed not only autonomy of economic activity for the Korean Chinese but also the freedom to choose to live in specific areas. However, since these changes in citizenship status were unaccompanied by the dramatic improvements in economic status many Korean Chinese people "choose" to live in areas where real estate prices are relatively low. Together, it is these tendencies that led to the formation of the enclave.

The enclave was a place where its inhabitants both lived and worked. Its resident Chinese Koreans were incorporated into industries close to their home (primarily the service industry), and in their free time enjoyed and consumed a variety of activities and goods. Because it was the place where almost all information related to life in Korea for Korean Chinese was collected and circulated – and was related services were provided, this led Korean Chinese people from other regions to visit the area, and become temporarily incorporated into its networks. All this meant that the enclave, with its permanent and flexible population of workers and consumers was a rich environment for business people.

Summary

In this chapter, we look carefully at the enclave. Korean Chinese in South Korea, whose legal status was stable and had guaranteed economic autonomy, chose their living area according to their economic status. They settled in an area in Seoul with low real estate prices and convenient transportation. The similar economic classes concentrated in the southwestern part created a particular economic market that, although similar to the general Korean market, had special demands. Korean Chinese with business experience noticed this, and they became the enclave entrepreneurs. The enclave provided the entrepreneurs with a stable supply of both labour and consumers, and was their economic/class foundation.

Note

1 The rapid increase of Chinese students in Korea has been affected by China's education policies, Korea's policies for attracting foreign students, and the admission policies of Korean Universities. Routes taken by Chinese Students to study abroad in Korea include (1) study abroad agencies, (2) sister universities, (3) the establishment of departments for joint research between Korea and China, (4) branch schools of Korean universities, and (5) personal applications. With the opening of the education market, famous universities in Korea have engineered their rise in institutional status by attracting foreign students as part of "internationalization (or globalization) projects", while rural universities are in a life-or-death struggle to attract foreign students to meet their student quotas.

References

2008 Factual Survey on the Satisfaction of Visiting and Employment System (2008FSSVES). 2008. Ministry of Justice and Ministry of Labor.

2013 Survey of Korean Chinese Living in Seoul (2013SKCLS). 2013. Seoul Metropolitan City.

Cho, Mi-Jeong, 2015. *A Study of Korean Chinese Elementary Students' Educational Status and Support in Korea* (in Korean). Master's thesis of Hankuk University of Foreign Studies.

Koo, Ha-Gen. 2002. *The Formation of Korean Working Class* (in Korean). Seoul: Changbi.

Korea Export Industry Corporation. 1994. *40 Years History of the Korea Export Industry Corporation* (in Korean). Seoul.

Lee, Sang-Cheol. 2012. "The Making of Exporting Industrial Complex and Its Transfiguration: Guro Industrial Complex (1963–1987)" (in Korean). *Donghyangwajeonmang* 85: 223–263.

Ministry of Public Administration and Security. 2008. *Foreign Residents in Local Provinces*. Seoul.

Ministry of Public Administration and Security. 2016. *Foreign Residents in Local Provinces*. Seoul.

Park, Gwang-Seong. 2006. *Labor Influx of Korean Chinese and Social Changes in Global Era* (in Korean). Doctoral Dissertation of Seoul National University.

Park, Woo. 2013. "The Determinants of Expected Stay Duration of Korean-Chinese Workers in Korea" (in Korean). *Studies of Koreans Abroad* 30: 163–183.

Park, Woo. 2015. "A Study on the Stratification of Korean Chinese Community" (in Korean). *Studies of Koreans Abroad* 37: 89–120.

Park, Woo et al. 2015. *A Study on Chinese Female Worker and Local Labor Market in South Korea* (in Korean). Seoul: Center for Labor Welfare of Guro District.

Seoul Geumcheon-gu. 1997. *A Local Newspaper of Culture of Geomcheon-gu* (in Korean). Seoul.

Seoul Guro-gu. 1997. *A Local Newspaper of Guro-gu* (in Korean). Seoul.

Son, Jeong-Sun. 2012. "The Bifurcation of Industrial Structure of Seoul Digital Complex's and Expansion of Peripheral Services" (in Korean). *Korean Journal of Labor Studies* 18(1): 273–310.

4 Entrepreneurs and entrepreneurship

There are various conditions for becoming an entrepreneur. These include an individual's education level, their human capital (such as their career history), their family or friendship network, capital, and a labour and consumption market. But the fulfillment of these conditions is not enough to explain the process of becoming an entrepreneur. To legally and practically be an entrepreneur, you must be the legal owner of a corporation. This is directly related to the legal status of the businessperson, as, in Korea, only citizenship or an equivalent legal status gives the right to own a corporation. Only when this status is attained could Korean Chinese in possession of resources fit for business become entrepreneurs.

Legal status

In South Korea, Korean Chinese's citizenship status has been regulated through a variety of policies. Until the early 2000s, Korean Chinese held the same status as other immigrants.[1] However, in 2004, the Overseas Koreans act was revised and from 2007 applied to ethnic Koreans from China and countries in the Commonwealth of Independent States (CIS). This meant they were recognized as legal "compatriots" and could qualify for different statuses to immigrants without Korean heritage.

The Overseas Korean status (*jaeoedongpo*) could be granted to Korean Chinese who had either abundant human, social or economic capital, or could work for an extended period in one of Korea's 3D (dirty, dangerous and difficult) industries. Immigrants with this status effectively possessed the same rights as South Korean citizens (bar the right to vote in elections or run for office), and could obtain South Korean citizenship fairly easily. The Foreign Korean Worker (*Dongponodongja*) status allowed Korean Chinese to work freely in secondary industries and opened up the possibility of obtaining Overseas Korean status. The Foreign Worker status gave people the chance to work in secondary industry under severe restrictions and prohibited participation in primary industries. These statuses directly decided the range of an individual's economic freedom. Korean Chinese Entrepreneurs did not enter the country with a status allowing them to start businesses. Instead, they had to proceed through a series of statuses until they finally reached the one that allowed them to start businesses. For some, this only involved changing status once, but for others it took five switches before that could be achieved.

Table 4.1 shows that certain statuses have been very attractive for Korean Chinese residents. At the time they entered South Korea 5.6% of entrepreneurs possessed Korean nationality, 6.5% had permanent resident status, and 3.2% were recognized as Overseas Koreans. Another 10.5% entered as foreign students, 10.5% on visiting employee visas, and 11.3% on spouse visas. The remainder (55.6%) entered with a variety of other statuses. At the time of the survey, however, 37.1% had South Korean nationality, 18.5% had permanent residency, and 36.3% had Overseas Korean status. Only 4.8% and 3.2% had visiting employment visas and spouse visas, respectively. Significantly, this means that while only 15.3% of Korean Chinese entered the country with statuses granting the right to own businesses (Korean nationality, Overseas Korean, or permanent residency), by the time of the survey, 91.9% had acquired that right through status changes. Among those surveyed, many also planned to change their status in the future, too, with 35.2% looking to acquire South Korean nationality, 48.9% permanent residency, and 4.5% Overseas Korean status. Only 11.4% were seeking other statuses. So it is clear that Korean Chinese businesses people were attracted to Korean nationality and statuses that, in practice, granted equivalent rights (see Table 4.1).[2]

The next task is to examine how business people changed their legal status. There are four main routes by which this was achieved, and they will be described one by one: the first being naturalization through South Korean relatives; the second being a change from "Foreign Worker" status to "Overseas Korean" status, the third being the acquisition of Overseas Korean Status or permanent residency rights through education levels, and the fourth being via marriage to a South Korean national.

Table 4.1 Current and planned status of entrepreneurs (Unit: %)

	Entry into South Korea (N = 124)	First Status Change (N = 85)	Second Status Change (N = 49)	Third Status Change (N = 18)	Fourth Status Change (N = 6)	Fifth Status Change (N = 3)	Current Status (N = 124)	Planned Change (N = 88)
National	5.6	17.6	20.4	0	50.0	0	37.1	35.2
Residence	6.5	2.4	14.3	0	0	0	18.5	48.9
Overseas Korean status	3.2	22.4	12.2	77.8	0	0	36.3	4.5
Visiting employment visa	10.5	24.7	16.3	0	0	0	4.8	0.0
Student visa	7.8	0	0	0	0	0	0	0
Marriage visa	11.3	2.3	14.3	16.7	50.0	100.0	3.2	0.0
Other (Inc. short term)	55.6	29.4	22.4	5.6	0	0	0.0	11.4

Source: 2013 Survey of Korean Chinese Living in Seoul.

Naturalization through South Korean relatives

Mr K, who runs the "Product L" business. His grandparents were born in Andong, Gyeongsangbuk-do. His parents are from Uljin-gun Gangwon-do, where his two older brothers were born. He isn't sure whether his older sister was born on the way to China, or in present-day Heilongjiang in Northern China. Since his parents migrated to China later in the Japanese colonial period, he was recognized by the South Korean government as a second-generation compatriot. After graduating high school in China, he was invited by his cousins to visit Korea for a short time in 1991 on a visiting visa for relatives. His relatives in China all ran businesses, and he followed their example before deciding to move to South Korea on a D-8 (corporate/foreign investor) visa. In 2006, he obtained South Korean nationality.

Ms Y, the owner of "G travel agency" and a second-generation compatriot, was born in Heilongjiang, China. Her father, originally from Daegu and a first-generation compatriot, remembers going to China as a child while her mother was born in China, probably in Pyeongan-do (which is now part of North Korea). Ms Y says that are many other people in Heilongjiang whose families come from the Gyeongsangbuk-do area. All her own close relatives were in South Korea, and it was through their invitation that she came to South Korea.

From "Foreign Worker" to "Overseas Korean"

Unlike Ms Y, the owner of the "S Chinese Lamb Shish Kebab" restaurant, Mr L did not have any close relatives in South Korea, so he had to pay a broker about 77,000 Yuan to facilitate his move to South Korea. Initially he had a C-2 visa, but after returning visiting China in 2000 he was only given a three-month visa when he returned. He stayed past this limit illegally. In mid-2000 however, the government introduced a policy through which he could legally obtain an E-9 visa, which he soon did. With this visa he was able to freely come and go. He then tried to apply for a D-8 investor's visa, but to do that he needed to prove that he had transferred money *from China* into the South Korean bank. In 2004, Mr L went back to China with the money he had earned in Korea, then re-entered with his money so that he could make the correct documents to get an investors visa. He now has Overseas Korean status.

H Travel Agency's owner Mr K also has no close relatives in South Korea. This meant it wasn't easy to come to South Korea. He used a fake passport from a broker to try to enter the country but was caught at the airport and was banned from the country for a long time. When the policy changed, he used his real passport to enter the country legally. He entered with a C-3 visa and did all kinds of work to support himself. He then changed to an investor's visa. However, he eventually changed to an F-4 resident's visa in 2004 because the restrictions on his business activity with an investor's visa were preventing him from expanding his business.

Acquisition of "Overseas Korean Status" or permanent residency rights by highly educated Korean Chinese

The owner of "trading company L", Mr K began studying for a PhD in Korea in 2003. As a student, he was in the country with a D-2 visa and was only was permitted to do part-time jobs, or any other activity besides studying, after obtaining authorization from the immigration office. After an initial two-year period, he had to extend for six months at a time, each time providing a provide a letter of recommendation from his supervisor, proof of bank balance along with other documents. However, from 2007, it became possible for Korean Chinese students studying above master's level to obtain Overseas Korean status, and Mr K immediately took this opportunity. He says that the most important advantage of Overseas Korean status is the freedom to start businesses.

The M Chinese Lamb Shish Kebab Restaurant's owner, Mr H, is a young businessman still in his 30s. After graduating from university in China, he gained a master's in business studies at a Korean university in 2004, before finding professional work. At first, he worked on an employee visa, but soon qualified for residency given his experience, education and, in particular, his long service at a single company. After six years of employment, he decided to set up his own company.

Acquisition of nationality through spouse

Ms K says that for people like her, that is, with no close relations in the country, it is hard to come to South Korea. This is why most women, including her, come to South Korea through marriage. Ms K, now the owner of "J Cold Noodles", married a Korean man after her first husband died. Sadly, not long after Ms K arrived in Busan (South Korea's second biggest city), her Korean husband also died, and she was subsequently refused South Korean nationality. After a complicated process, her marriage was finally recognized, and she was able to become a naturalized citizen.

"Q Chinese Restaurant" is owned by Ms P, who acquired South Korean nationality in 2001 through her marriage to a Korean citizen.

Ms P didn't gain citizenship immediately after her marriage though, and reports that this caused her some complicated problems, as she had to live in the country under "visiting cohabitation (F-1)" visa. She had to put up with the government regularly checking whether she was still living her husband – probably part of the government's measures to uncover marriage fraud. Two years after her marriage, she finally gained South Korean nationality and could live with the same freedoms as any other citizen.

From these short accounts we can see that while entrepreneurs followed different routes to change their citizenship status, there is at least one point of commonality. They have moved from statuses with limited economic freedom and have either become citizens or gained statuses that give equivalent economic rights. For Korean Chinese in South Korea, citizenship status determines economic freedom – the access one has to one's own capital and whether one has the right to maximize its use.

Resource

Human capital

Although the Korean Chinese entrepreneurs we have encountered in this study have various occupational backgrounds, experience in professional, business, and service roles are particularly well represented (see Table 4.2). These experiences in China were important to the entrepreneurs' future businesses in South Korea.

Due to their experience and careers in China the entrepreneurs considered working in South Korea's secondary labour market "difficult" and "unappealing" (see Table 4.3). At the same time, however, they were "prohibited" from participating in the primary labour market, reporting that it was nearly "impossible" because their education level is generally lower than Korean Chinese professions (see Table 4.4).

Table 4.2 Entrepreneurs' work experience and main occupation (Unit: %)

	Business	Employee in Service Industry	White Collar	Others
Work experience (N = 124)	31.8	13.1	33.6	22.3
Main occupation (N = 117)	47.0	7.7	32.4	12.9

Source: 2013 Survey of Korean Chinese Living in Seoul.

Note: Work experience refers to all jobs the respondents have had in China. Main occupation refers to the participant's most important occupation in China.

Table 4.3 Entrepreneurs' motivation (Unit: %)

Motivations	Percentage (N = 124)
Continuing occupation from life in China	26.6
Difficulty finding white-collar work in Korea	8.1
Other work is difficult and unappealing	33.9
Suitable for my aptitude	32.3

Source: 2013 Survey of Korean Chinese Living in Seoul.

Table 4.4 Entrepreneurs' education level (white-collar and blue-collar comparison) (Unit: %)

	Blue Collar		White Collar	Entrepreneur	
	2013 (N = 430)[a]	2008 (N = 996)[b]	2013 (N = 118)[a]	2013 (N = 124)[a]	2008 (N = 200)[c]
High school level or less	79.3	91.1	22.3	58.0	73.5
Vocational college or above	20.7	8.9	77.7	42.0	26.5

Notes
a 2013 Survey of Korean Chinese Living in Seoul.
b 2008 Factual Survey on the Satisfaction of Visiting and Employment System.
c 2008 Survey on the Korean Chinese Enclave.

Family support

In the early stages of a business, the support and involvement of family members, including children, was also important. Eighty-eight of the 124 entrepreneurs had children, and in 43.2% of cases where there was one child in the family this child lived together with the entrepreneur in South Korea. For families with two children, this rate rose to 75.0%. This means that most entrepreneurs with children brought them to South Korea. Most (81.6%) of the entrepreneurs' spouses also lived in South Korea (the remaining 18.4% lived in China). 47.7% of entrepreneurs lived with their spouses and all their children in South Korea, a higher rate than both general workers (20.9%) and professionals (34.8%) (2013SKCLS).

Initial capital

The start-up capital used by the entrepreneurs was secured in various ways. Most came from money earned and saved in South Korea, but some entrepreneurs also brought savings from China, either to supplement their Korean savings, or as the main source. In some cases, money earned in Korea was transferred to China before being returned to Korea. In other cases, entrepreneurs sold their property in China to raise capital. A relatively high proportion of start-up capital also came from money borrowed from friends or relatives. 7.3% of entrepreneurs used bank loans to fund their start-up costs (see Table 4.5).

Since most businesses were small, the initial investment amount was generally not large, less than 20 million won in 39.6% of cases and 20–50 million won for 47.8% of the businesses. In around 10% of businesses the start-up costs fell between 50 and 100 million won. Only 2% of the businesses required more than 100 million won to set up (see Table 4.6). It may be that the growth of the service industry in Korean Chinese areas is partly down to the low start-up costs it involved.[3]

Table 4.5 Preparation of investment capital (Unit: %)

Funding Method	Percentage (N = 124)
Personal savings	75.0
Transfer of funds from China to Korea	26.6
Selling property owned in China	9.7
Transfer of Korean funds to China and back again	4.8
Borrowing from relatives	14.5
Borrowing from friends	12.1
Bank loan	7.3
Private loan	0.0

Source: 2008 Survey on the Korean Chinese Enclave.

Table 4.6 Amount of investment capital (Unit: %)

	Chinese Nationality	Korean Nationality	Total
Less than 20 million won	40.3	39.1	39.6
20–50 million won	44.4	50.1	47.8
50–100 million won	8.3	9.2	8.8
100–200 million won	1.4	0.0	1.0
200–300 million won	1.4	0.0	1.0
Total	100.0 (N = 72)	100.0 (N = 87)	100.0 (N = 159)

Source: 2008 Survey on the Korean Chinese Enclave.

So we have seen in this section that the majority of Korean Chinese entrepreneurs have experience running businesses in China, or have relatively experience helpful for running a business. Their education level falls between the level of Korean Chinese in the primary and secondary labour markets, encouraging the choice to set up businesses. Most were supported by family when they began their business and required small amounts of initial investment capital. So compared to Korean Chinese in professional jobs and the secondary labour market, these people possessed capital more suitable for starting a small business.

Interdependency of status and resource

At foundation

Ms K, the owner of "J Cold Noodles" who came to Korea through marriage to a Korean national before acquiring Korean nationality, used her business experience in China to set up a buggy restaurant in Wangsimni, Seoul with money transferred over from China. After a short time, the restaurant had to be demolished to make way for road construction. She received around 30 million won compensation for this. While she was considering what to do for her next business, she attended a university reunion event in Garibong-dong and noticed how many Korean Chinese lived in the area. At that time, there weren't many restaurants in Garibong-dong, and she recalls people lining up outside what restaurants there were to eat food tasting of home. More unexpectedly, she witnessed Koreans too coming to eat Chinese food. She decided to open a cold noodle restaurant in the area in 2005. Ms K's business was a relatively early arrival in Garibong-dong, and she already had experience in this sector. Her business grew day by day, and she now owns five restaurants in the area. Although Ms K did not acquire South Korean nationality in order in start a business, the rights it provides opened the possibility for her to utilize the experience and capital she earned in China.

The owner of "G Travel Agent", Mrs Y, acquired Korean nationality after coming to the country at the invitation of family. She did quite a few different jobs in her first years in the country but says her experience as a life insurance salesman was most important. While most of the customers were Korean there were some Korean Chinese as well, and one of them asked whether she would like to try running a travel agency. Seeking a challenge, she took over her customer's travel agency. She says that 99% of the customers coming to her first travel agency were Korean Chinese. One advantage of her new venture was that the set up and running cost of a travel agency was less than he expected – her first office cost a little less than 30 million won including key money, and she estimates that that would be a little less than normal. She now runs travel agencies in China and Korea with her husband. Because Mrs Y was able to acquire South Korean nationality, she was able to work at a large (and prestigious) insurance company. Moreover, because she became a citizen, she didn't face any regulatory obstacles setting up her travel agency. This meant she could set up her business with a modest (small, even) amount of capital. Her South Korean nationality, low start-up cost, and strong family support had a positive impact on the start of her business.

After acquiring South Korean nationality in 2005 Mr L, who has a Chinese Master's degree and runs "Newspaper H", worked at a government-affiliated institution working with foreign labourers. At that time, the main topic of conversation at their meetings was the number of crimes committed by Korean Chinese and other non-Koreans in the country. Mr L felt that since misdemeanours were more common than violent crimes, the rate could be reduced through education about South Korea's laws and better communication. This was his motivation to band together with friends and invest 15 million won to set up a newspaper focused on legal issues. The friends were all studying for, or had already finished, their PhDs. It was a case of highly educated Korean Chinese with South Korean nationality investing a small amount of money to establish a newspaper.

"Restaurant C" is owned by Mr O. He came to South Korea in 2003 and obtained nationality two years later. He combined all the money he had in South Korea with money from China to give him 400 million won to use to set up a large, upmarket restaurant. Since setting up a business alone has many risks in Korea, he went into business with a close Korean friend who had experience running a business in Shenyang, China. The business is in Mr O's name, but the Korean partner helped with various legal matters. In this case, a naturalized Korean Chinese with the necessary capital has used the Korean affiliates to start a business.

Business expansion and changes

Mr S, who came to South Korea after graduating middle school in Korea, now runs the "S Chinese Lamb Shish Kebab Restaurant". When he was younger, he was involved in an accident while working for a small business in Sihwa Industrial Complex. This left him in an awkward position afterwards since he was remaining in the country illegally and found it hard to find a new job. It was at this point he was given the chance to run a Chinese lamb shish kebab restaurant whose owner had to suddenly leave the country. Because of the circumstances, he only had to pay ten million won for the business but was not able to actually own the restaurant until his presence in the country became legal. The restaurant did well, and he was able to expand the premises before opening a second branch and a third branch outside Daerim-dong. Mr L is representative of cases in which Korean Chinese after gaining Overseas Korean status in South Korea come to own a business they have been running but have been unable to officially own because of their legal status.

Mr N, who began the business after being granted residency rights in South Korea, owns "C Travel & Management Company". The company employed lawyers, accountants, and other professionals to assist ethnic Koreans without citizenship through administrative and legal issues they might encounter in the country. He says that he didn't have any issues putting together the capital required to start the business. He did have issues trying to obtain Overseas Korean status, however, since he hadn't received higher education in China; fortunately, he was granted residency rights thanks to the amount of money he had been able to save up in Korea and his business activities. To expand the business, Mr N had to employ a lot of young, talented people because of the specialist nature of the business he had set up. However, he found that it was difficult to do this with just residency rights and so decided to apply for naturalization. He was successful and is now a Korean citizen. For Mr N, legal status played a key role in the foundation and expansion of his businesses, having started the business on being granted residency and then seeking citizenship in order to expand the company.

"M Logistics" Ms P came to South Korea with Overseas Korean status before setting up a cosmetics purchasing agent business. She joined together with a number of other people doing similar business in order to take advantage of Korean cosmetics brands in China by exporting on a large scale. The group then decided that it would be a good idea to buy a small cosmetics manufacturer in Korea, form a corporation, develop a trademark, and export the finished products to China. However, when they tried to do this, she faced a series of problems – especially securing finance from the bank – because of her legal status in the country. This led her to apply for Korean citizenship. In other words, Ms P sought to become a naturalized South Korean because, even though she was able to own a business, there were limitations on her economic activities when she tried to expand her ventures.

Ms S is the owner of "Y Cellphone Dealer". In 2009, she was running a small store after receiving Overseas Korean status. The thought of investing a small amount in a coffee shop or a restaurant franchise began to appeal to her, but then she began to consider investing in something completely different from her current venture. This is why she decided to set up a cell phone dealership when she discovered that there weren't many in Daerim-Dong. Around 2005, she says there were cell phone stores run by Koreans but almost none run by Korean Chinese. She thought that it would be easier to deal with Korean telecommunication companies and cell phone manufacturers if she had Korean nationality rather than Overseas Korean status. So when she started a new business, she also changed her nationality to South Korean.

To summarize what we have found in this section, even where the entrepreneurs had the necessary financial and practical resources to own and run a business, this was not enough for them to be the legal and actual owner of said business. Rather, the fundamental possibility of establishing and running a business was citizenship status, that is, the legal status of a citizen or a citizen, provided that the core possibility of establishing and owning a business was provided by citizenship or a status offering the equivalent rights (such as the Overseas Korean status). Their resources could only be put to full use once they had secured a guarantee of their legal status in the country. Legal status played a key role when entrepreneurs were looking to expand their business or move into a new field, when they wanted to become the actual owner of a business they had been running and when they needed secure loans from financial institutions.

Service industry

The policy changes relating to Korean Chinese's legal status in 2007 led to the diversification of businesses in areas heavily populated by Korean Chinese (see Table 4.7). In the restaurant industry, various kinds of premises appeared, from large general restaurants selling all kinds of dishes to small restaurants specializing in a single dish, as well as fast food restaurants. In the distribution industry, Korean Chinese entrepreneurs dominated the distribution of Chinese made goods not only to Korean Chinese areas of the city but also to other areas of the country too. Within the Korean Chinese areas, they mainly supplied Chinese products, including food, to traditional markets, supermarkets, and restaurants. Travel agencies not only worked

Table 4.7 Business type (Unit: %)

Business Type	2013SKCLS (N = 124)	2013SBG (N = 61)
Restaurant	37.8	62.2
Karaoke	14.0	16.4
Cell phone dealer	2.0	1.6
Clothing store	1.3	1.6
Computer store	1.3	–
Chinese produce store	3.3	–
Off-license	0.7	–
Trade company	12.7	–
Travel agency	11.0	8.2
Cosmetics store	2.0	–
Other	6.0	–
Massage	–	3.3
Administration company	–	3.3
Beauty and nail Salons	–	3.3

Source: 2013 Survey of Korean Chinese Living in Seoul, 2013 Survey on the Business of Garibong-dong.

Note: In the wide-area survey, some entrepreneurs owned more than one business, so the total is not 100%.

to attract tourists and arrange holidays but also as intermediary institutions helping to solve the problem that face Korean Chinese living in South Korea, particularly through their role in mediating changes in citizenship and organizing the invitation of relatives into the country. Business people sold various products. As the demand for electronic devices like cell phones and computers in Korean Chinese residential areas increased, electronics stores and cell phone dealers appeared to meet it. There was also a growth in clothing and cosmetics stores and small businesses like pubs, karaoke rooms, and massage parlours.

Catering

Non-specialist restaurants

Non-specialist restaurants serve 20 to 30 dishes. We can categorize these restaurants by size according to the number of 8–10-seater tables they have. Restaurants with less than five or fewer tables are categorized here as small restaurants, medium-sized restaurants have between five and nine of these tables, and large restaurants have ten or more. The restaurants usually employ more than one professional chef, and the large ones have a luxurious interior and a large staff. The menu is made up of dishes from Northern, particularly Northeastern, regions of

China, as this is where the majority of Chinese nationals and Korean Chinese in South Korea come from. Depending on the size of the restaurants, they may also host birthday parties and wedding receptions. Normally, any kind of banquet or party is held in the medium-sized or larger restaurants. Because there are many Korean Chinese who settle down as family units, it is more convenient to gather in South Korea than to go to China when there is a holiday or a family event.

Specialist restaurants

Specialist restaurants have a main specialty that is accompanied on the menu by a few other options. Chinese-style lamb shish kebab and hotpot (*shabu-shabu*) are typical specialties. The lamb kebabs were originally eaten in provinces like Xinjiang and Inner Mongolia, but spread to the Korean Chinese communities in Northeast China, who adapted them to suit their taste. Korean Chinese began to open lamb kebab restaurants in South Korea after they became popular in Yanbian in the 1990s. Lamb and mutton is almost never used in Korea cooking and demand for the meat in South Korea rose in tandem with the Korean Chinese population. According to L, the owner of the S Lamb Kebab Restaurant, "At first, restaurants used lambs raised in Chungcheong and Gangwon – provinces that were not too far from Seoul. However, as the demand for lamb grew, the lambs from Australia and New Zealand were imported".

The main ingredients of hotpots are lamb and beef. They are not, despite their importance in the Korean Chinese restaurant industry, originally a Korean Chinese recipe. They were adapted from Szechwan and Inner Mongolian dishes to suit Chinese Korean tastes. Because the culture in China is to order a variety of dishes even if there is a "main dish" customers order a selection of dishes. When considered as a single restaurant, these are small operations. However, it appears to be better to expand these businesses by opening branches in other locations rather than expanding the original premises.

Korean Chinese restaurants

Korean Chinese restaurants, as you might expect, mainly offer traditional Korean Chinese cuisine. Traditional Korean Chinese is broadly the same as Korean food but it does have some unique local characteristics. Yanbian chilled noodles is a classic example of a Korean Chinese dish and is a popular choice in the enclave's Korean Chinese restaurants. But as this is a seasonal (hot weather) dish, the restaurants have to offer different kinds of foods. The owner of "J Chilled Noodles" reported that

customers mainly come to us from early summer to early fall. They stop coming if the weather is cold. So while we offer chilled noodles as our main specialty, we also have to make hot noodle soups and other Chinese dishes in both the summer and winter.

(J Chilled Noodles, Mrs K)

Small restaurants

The small restaurants operating in the enclave generally have less than five 4-seater tables and don't tend to generate much of a profit. They make simple, easy-to-eat rice soups and other rice-based dishes that attract a variety of customers. People employed in the secondary labour market, especially temporary workers coming in to the restaurants on the way home after finishing work, are particularly common visitors. For those who do manual labour, it is often more expedient to eat simple food in these restaurants rather than cooking when they get home. And as these establishments don't chase big profits, the price is very reasonable for workers. Mr K from Y restaurant observed that

Korean Chinese men enjoy pork *silaji jangmul* [a kind of rice soup made with dried greens]. We just make it as you would at home and people often come to eat it. There's a lot of places to eat rice soup in Korea, but you need to eat something that tastes of home, don't you?

Chinese fast food restaurants

This category includes street food. People lined up outside the stores selling Chinese baked goods that began to appear in Daerim 2-dong a few years ago. Their pastries, made from cereals like wheat flour, corn flour, and mung bean flour, are popular snacks. Besides pastries, twisted doughnuts, red-bean paste filled rolls, and different kinds of steamed buns are on offer. When there is a surge in customers these businesses can make a good profit, but normally they just break even. There is also meat-based street food – dishes made from various parts of a pig's head as well as pork trotters and sausages. There are poultry dishes available too. Goose and duck can be found along with chicken feet and drumsticks. These foods can be made in a small outlet or in restaurants that serve them along with their main specialties. The customers for street food are diverse.

Distribution businesses

Distributors

Corporate distributors appeared around 2005. Their main customers are restaurants and catering establishments. The distribution company procures finished goods from the general markets of China or Korea and delivers them to Korean Chinese businesses. Mr K from L Product describes how they started their business and where it is heading:

> We really got into the logistics business in 2005. We found that Chinese food products were being brought into Korea in carry-on luggage to bypass customs clearance ... Currently, we distribute 50–60 different kinds of finished Chinese food products in Korea. Chinese sauces, tofu, sesame sauce, and noodles. The things we deal with are aimed at the needs of hotels that serve Chinese food and Korean Chinese. But 80%–90% of our customers are actually Chinese. There are already about 500,000 Chinese in Korea and this number is likely to increase to one million in the future. These are our target customers.

Although the distribution companies import finished products, they need to be adapted to meet the demands of the Korean market. Mr K explained,

> we import agricultural products and seafood in large bags. It is different for each company, but the garlic that I bring in comes in 20–50 kg packages, and other agricultural products also packed in large quantities. If you want to distribute this to markets or marts in Korea you need to open up the package and put it into smaller bags. You have to put garlic in bags of 200–500 g, for example, and it's the just same for seafood.

Businessmen involved in trade businesses also prepare Korean products for export to China.

Chinese food stores

Chinese food stores mainly deal with products imported from China such as liquor, confectionery, processed agricultural products, processed foods, seasonings, and snacks. The most common Chinese confectionery is the moon cake, a snack eaten at thanksgiving in China. There are also breads and other confectioneries, as well as the salted duck eggs and other salted food products popular in China. These grocery stores sell the Chinese food products imported by the distribution companies described above.

The general mart

In addition to daily necessities, the general mart stocks groceries and other foodstuff. Korean Chinese traders repackage and deliver Chinese agricultural products to these general stores. Chinese consumers also access Chinese agricultural products such as garlic, onion, leek, Chinese cabbage, and bracken through these marts, which are run by both Koreans and Korean Chinese. Through these marts, both consumers and mart owners are connected to the Korean Chinese distribution companies.

Travel agencies

Travel agencies provided services such as attracting and sending tourists, ticket sales, and administrative services. In the case of attracting and sending tourists, agencies from Hong Kong, Taiwan and those run by Koreans were already established in the Korea-China tourism industry. So Korean Chinese entrepreneurs who started businesses in the mid and late 2000s needed to invest a lot to make a presence for their enterprises in the market. They developed new products such as offline ticket sales and administrative services to give themselves an edge. These services were aimed at the many Korean Chinese past middle age who were not used to accessing online services. They could purchase ferry or airplane tickets with cash in Korean Chinese tourist agencies. It was simply more convenient for older customers to visit a travel agency, speak directly to an agent, and pay in cash than to go through the rigmarole of connecting to the internet, searching for the departure and arrival times, comparing the prices, and then making the purchase online, especially as there weren't really suitable places to print e-tickets.

One common problem faced by Korean Chinese residents and other Chinese nationals was the visa issue. In order to get a visa, they had to visit the immigration office, complete the application form, draw a waiting ticket, and then wait in the queue. Of course, with online reservation service, there was no longer any need to wait in line at the immigration office from dawn, but, nevertheless, the large population of Chinese nationals meant that even with an appointment, the process took a lot of time and effort. In response, Korean Chinese travel agencies began to offer visa application services. Moreover, the South Korean alien registration card must be issued within 90 days of new entry, has to be extended when nearing its expiration date, and must be updated whenever the owner begins a new job. There are other tasks that have to be dealt with at the immigration office too, all of which can be troublesome. If you pay a small fee to the agencies to do these tasks for you, then you can work instead of waiting in line at the immigration office.

Since the process for inviting family members to Korea is complicated and awkward, travel agencies also provide services to assist with this process. Mrs Y from G Travel Agency recounts helping one lady bring her entire family to South Korea:

> I remember meeting one grandmother. She had already acquired Korean nationality. She wanted to bring her son, her daughter, her daughter-in-law, her whole family, even her grandchildren. When she first came I explained the expenses and the steps she had to take in Korea. But she was very worried. Worried that the procedure would go wrong and her family wouldn't be able to come over. She came back with her daughter in-law and I spent three hours giving the exact same explanation again. After listening the daughter-in-law said she would give it a go and started the process. Anyway, they were lucky and all twelve of the family were able to come to Korea and even got residency rights. When 12 people move to Korea, it's not just a matter of coming over – it costs a lot of money. Even just the processing fee was a nice income for us.

Around the year 2010, some travel agencies developed a new service called "medical tourism". They recruited people who wanted cosmetic surgery, medical check-ups, or treatments in and brought them to official medical institutions in Korea.

Sales businesses

Electronics stores

The electronics store sells electronic products and offer repair services. In the early days of migration, people's stay in Korean was limited, so they tended to favour cheap computers that they felt comfortable just throwing away once they had to leave the country. The enclave's electronic stores mainly sold used computer for this reason. However, as the number of permanent residents increased, so too did the demand for new notebooks and other electronics. Consumers did go to the large electronics markets in places like Yongsan, but some thought there was no need to go so far if they could find quality-guaranteed products in the vicinity of the enclave. These stores also sell parts for those who wanted to build their own PCs.

Mobile phone stores

Mobile phone stores started to appear in the enclave from around 2010 after the rules restricting foreigners from setting up contracts with telecom companies were relaxed. Until the mid-2000s, it was almost impossible to get a phone contract with a foreign student visa or an industrial worker visa. As Korean Chinese have changed their legal status in the country, new sign-ups have become possible under their own name, and Korean Chinese have been able to get phone contracts more easily than before. As a result, Korean Chinese who understood the demand this would create and were able to run a business moved quickly to establish mobile phone stores and started to do business with the local residents.

Cosmetics and clothing stores

Korean cosmetics and clothing are popular products in China. As well as exporting to China entrepreneurs set up stores in the enclave. The convenience of being able to purchase goods in your residence or work area, even if you did not go to a department store, appealed to the customers who come to these stores. Like other cosmetic stores, they sell a variety of products and brands. The clothing stores mainly offer everyday clothes rather than designer items. They offer used clothes too, which are mainly purchased by male workers employed in manufacturing or construction.

Other sectors

Small bars

These small bars normally have three to five tables. Workers living in the area enjoy them because they can drink at cheap prices, but they almost never expand and ownership changes hands regularly.

Korean karaoke bars

We cannot omit karaoke rooms when discussing Korean Chinese culture. In the early 1990s, nightlife such as "Karaoke" was introduced to the Korean Chinese community in China. It became customary to go to karaoke to relax a little after staff dinners. Some of the karaoke rooms operated by Korean Chinese were taken over from Korean owners, and some were newly established. They offer a variety of music including Korean songs, Chinese songs, and songs from Yanbian.

Beauty industry

Mr P from Y Beauty Salon remarked that

> customers in salons need to communicate their desired style to the hairdresser but many people feel frustrated by the language barrier when they try to do this in places run by Koreans. I'm not sure but perhaps that's why a lot of Han Chinese and people who can't speak Korean well come to our salon.

The beauty salons found in the enclave are generally small, local places used mostly by middle-aged women and male workers looking for simple haircuts. There are also nail bars and other small places offering beauty treatments.

Massage parlours

Massage parlours offer foot rubs, meridian massages, and *chuna*. They have a diverse customer base and, in particular, offer low-cost services for people doing manual jobs.

Class position

The increase in Korean Chinese entrepreneurs changed the composition of business ownership in the areas studied. A 2008 survey of businesses with signs in just Chinese or in both Chinese and Korean found that 44.8% had naturalized Korean Chinese owners, 37.1% were owned by Korean Chinese with Chinese nationality, and only 13.4% were owned by South Koreans (2008SKCE).[4]

The Korean Chinese neighbourhoods provided a base for the entrepreneurs. Even those with businesses outside these areas had almost always started the initial business within these areas before expanding outwards. We can see this in Table 4.9, which shows that 97.5% of the business owners started their first business within a Korean Chinese neighbourhood.

Table 4.8 Business locations (Unit: %)

	First Business (N = 118)	Second Business (N = 33)	Third Business (N = 15)	Fourth Business (N = 7)
Enclave	97.5	74.8	46.7	100.0
Other	2.5	15.2	53.3	0.0

Source: 2013 Survey of Korean Chinese Living in Seoul.

This number rate fell for second businesses, of which 74.8% were located inside an enclave, and even more for third businesses – which were set up outside of Korean Chinese neighbourhoods about half the time (46.7% inside and 53.3% outside) (see Table 4.8).

Mr L.'s business expansion demonstrates nicely how this process plays out. He founded his second restaurant (the "Q Hotpot Restaurant") in the same Korean Chinese neighbourhood of Daerim 1-dong as his first restaurant (the "S Chinese Lamb Kebab Restaurant"). For his third restaurant, however, Mr L chose a location outside the Korean Chinese neighbourhood, in Yonggang-dong, Mapo-gu. He then made the first two restaurants into a franchise and handed control of them to another person (who is also Korean Chinese). Then, in 2016, he opened a fourth restaurant (his third Chinese Lamb Kebab restaurant) in the prosperous Yeoksam district of Gangnam.

The entrepreneurs hired people from the worker-rich Korean Chinese neighbourhoods. This ranged from one to fourteen people, and 82.3% were on salaries. Of the 124 entrepreneurs 61 had one or more family members among their employees. These 61 employers employed 108 family members in total, and 66.7% of these 108 family members were on salaries while 33.3% were unpaid. The entrepreneurs have fashioned various forms of employments, such as self-employment, family employment and salaried work to accord with the nature of the resources and capital they could mobilize (see Table 4.9). In addition to Korean Chinese

Table 4.9 Number of employees (Units: Person, %)

Type of Employment (N = 124)			Total Salaried Employees (N = 114)	
Self-employment	Total Employees			
10 (8.1%)	1–4	Over 5	1–4	Over 5
	77 (67.7%)	18 (16.2%)	94 (82.3%)	20 (9.7%)

Source: 2013 Survey of Korean Chinese Living in Seoul.

Note: The highest number of salaried employees for one business was 14. Because of missing data, the total does not equal 100%.

workers, they also employed Han Chinese and Korean workers. These employer-employee relations were formed through various recruitment and job search networks. With its guaranteed freedom to participate in the secondary labour market, Korean Chinese labour not only entered the Korea labour market but also formed a new labour market (enclave) working for business people in the Korean Chinese neighbourhoods of Seoul.[5]

The average earnings of the entrepreneurs were diverse (see Table 4.10). While there were entrepreneurs taking home less than two million won a month, some were earning more than ten million won per month. What is clear is that according to income the entrepreneurs had a higher economic status than workers, meaning that society in the Korean Chinese neighbourhoods was divided into at least two classes: worker and entrepreneur.

Mr L., the owner of "L Lamb Shish Kebab Restaurant" says that "last year (2012) one store raised at least ten million won per month. This varies a little according the location. If the location is good and things go well it goes up". Mr S, from the "S Corporation", observed that "things have kept going well since I started doing business. If you put all my stores together then my income last year (2012) was a few billion won. The CEO of "M Corporation", who was elected as the second president of Korea-China Entrepreneurs Management Association in 2016, has six stores under his direct and 15 franchise stores in Seoul and the surrounding metropolitan area. Just for the stores under his direct management the average total annual sales revenue was around six billion won, and the average annual sales revenue of each store, including the franchises was over 700 million won (*Yonhap News* 27 June 2016).

Entrepreneurs formed a service economy in Korean Chinese neighbourhoods and are the focus of this economy. Citizenship status allowed the entrepreneurs to utilize their resources by providing legal

Table 4.10 Average monthly income (Unit: %)

Category	Less than 1 Million Won	1–2 Million Won	2–3 Million Won	3–4 Million Won	4–5 Million Won	Over 5 Million Won	Total
Entrepreneur	0.0	28.8	17.1	17.1	13.5	23.4	100.0 (N = 110)
Salaried employee	4.3	69.6	19.0	5.5	1.5	0.1	100.0 (N = 392)

Source: 2013 Survey of Korean Chinese Living in Seoul.

and institutional guarantees. It also allowed them to hire labour from these populations. Meanwhile, the legal status of Korean Chinese not only guarantees their incorporation into Korea's secondary labour market but also allows them to be hired by Korean Chinese entrepreneurs. The Korean Chinese enclave service economy, formed through the legal status of Korean Chinese, was a complex network of employer-employee and production-consumption relations (mostly) between Korean Chinese entrepreneurs and Korean Chinese workers but involving Han Chinese and South Korean workers.

Summary

The entrepreneurs ran a variety of businesses, including restaurants, travel agencies, and trading companies. Entrepreneurs were able to mobilize their resources to set up businesses only after securing the rights to economic autonomy granted by citizenship or a status offering equivalent rights. They established small- and medium-sized businesses in the enclave and hired labour, situating them in the petite bourgeoisie "class" position – a pre-eminent economic/class position within the enclave's Korean Chinese population. And this position was the genesis of their effort to become the enclave's leading group as well as their practices aimed at acquiring equal status in Korean society.

Notes

1 Their status was regulated by a series of policies including the Industrial Trainee System, the Training Employment System, the Employment Management System, and the Employment Permission System.
2 See Park (2011) for details of South Korea's evolving policy on immigrants and Overseas Koreans.
3 Since 2010, there has been an increase in the number of people who start their businesses with a relatively large amount of capital.
4 And some other Chinese style foods such as noodles and dumplings.
5 Please refer to the Seoul History Museum (2013) for more information on businesses in the Garibong-dong Uma Gil commercial district.

References

2008 Survey on the Korean Chinese Enclave (2008SKCE). 2008. Overseas Korean Foundation.
2008 Factual Survey on the Satisfaction of Visiting and Employment System (2008FSSVES). 2008. Ministry of Justice and Ministry of Labor.
2013 Survey of Korean Chinese Living in Seoul (2013SKCLS). 2013. Seoul Metropolitan City.

2013 Survey on the Business of Garibong-dong (2013SBG). Unpublished raw data.

Park, Woo. 2011. "A Study on the Transition of Korean Chinese 'Organization' and Struggle for Recognition in Korea" (in Korean). *Economy and Society* 19: 239–265.

Seoul History Museum. 2013. *From Hinterland of Guro Export Industrial Complex to Multicultural Space: Garibong-dong* (in Korean). Seoul.

Yonhap News. 27 June 2016. "The Second Period of Success for Korean Chinese Compatriots: Seo Yong Gyu's Lamb Skewer Boom and Bust Story" (in Korean).

5 Organizations

From the early 1990s, Korean churches considered changing the legal status of Foreign Workers and Korean Chinese to be an important project, and as such, church-led groups were among the earliest organizations to speak for the enclave's Chinese Koreans. With the stabilization of Chinese Koreans' legal status, a class of entrepreneurs based in the enclave emerged. This group utilized their economic/class status in a drive to become the enclave community's leaders and representatives. In this chapter, we will examine the church-led merchant organizations of the early period and the later entrepreneur organizations.

The birth of merchant organizations

The organization of the Korean Chinese merchant was directly influenced by a religious body called the Korean Chinese Welfare Mission Centre (KCWMC, *joseonjokbogjiseongyoseinteo*). On 15 October 2000, the Korean Mission Policy Research Center set up the KCWMC in Uijuro Church in Hongje-dong, Seoul and elected Pastor Y to be its first director. Pastor Y was a member of the Korean Christians' Committee on Human Rights and was involved in the democratization movement. In February 1999, Pastor Y set up the Preparatory Committee for the KCWMC and gave scholarships to Korean Chinese students in South Korea and Yanbian. Many of those who participated at the centre at this time belonged to the council for Korean Chinese victims of fraud. (*Kukmin Ilbo* 18 October 2000). Pastor Y and his religious organization helped to form the very first Korean Chinese group, the Korean Chinese Association (KCA, *joseonjokyeonhabhoe*). This group began life on the 23 April 2000 and stated that its purpose was to "strengthen the friendship and solidarity among Korean Chinese residents in Korea, work towards better relation between China and Korea, and improve the status of Korean Chinese" (KCA 2010).

Mrs C was born in 1940 in Hailin, Heilongjiang Province and spent her early years in Yanbian. She came to Korea between late 1989 and early 1990 using a Korean broker. Although she didn't have any real family in Korea, the broker was able to help her pretend to be visiting a relative. This was before the re-establishment of diplomatic ties between South Korea and China so she had to travel to South Korea via Hong Kong. She left from Yanji, taking a train to Tianjin and then another to Guangzhou, where she stayed for a couple of days before travelling to Shenzhen by bus. Korean brokers told her every day that the visa problem would be solved in near future, so she had to stay and wait for the visa at Shenzhen for several days. She carried a lot of medicinal products like wild ginseng, and antlers with her on this journey – goods that were being smuggled between Hong Kong and Shenzhen. C purchased 30,000 yuan worth of these products before she left Yanji. All in all, it cost about 50,000 yuan to get to Seoul. And at this time in China people were considered wealthy if they had over 10,000 yuan in wealth or assets (*wanyuanhu*), so it was a significant investment. She stayed in Hong Kong for a few more days before finally arriving at Gimpo Airport in Seoul. Her visa provided her with three months in the country, and she began to sell her medicinal products on the street. There were a lot of other medicine peddlers though, and although she was able to sell all her stock, she wasn't even able to recoup their original cost. She ended up overstaying her visa. One problem was that people promised to pay for the medicine on a certain day and only gave her part of the money that day. It took a long time to collect all the money she was owed. In 1991, selling medicinal products on the street was banned, so she moved into the subway stations. She set up her store on the floor in the entrances and passages of City Hall Station and Seoul Station, with her goods laid out and labelled properly. At that time, most people in South Korea from China were from Heilongjiang Province, traced their roots to Gyeongsang-do ("do" meaning provincial administrative district of Korea), and had close relatives in South Korea. People from Yanbian had only just started to appear. Because her business wasn't going well, she let people who looked in serious need of medicinal products use her products on the understanding that they would pay later. She believes that there were surely many other merchants in the area who struggled to get back all the money they were owed.

Her products, all from Yanji, were things said to be good for the body, like wild ginseng, antler, woohwang cheongsimhwan (*niuhuang-qingxinwan*), and diet tea. Cheongsimhwan sold best. She bought it at a discount direct from a medicine factory and could sell one pack of six pills for 50,000 won in Seoul. In Yanji the same amount only sold for 28–30 yuan, which, given that 10,000 Korean won was worth 100 Chinese yuan, was a good profit. Her wild ginseng was brought in to the country by the smugglers whole rather than processed. Transactions were all in cash and it was a period of economic prosperity in Korea – she was able to pay the broker who helped her into the country within six months. Because she was staying without permission, she wasn't able to open a bank account or freely transfer money to China. She had to carry a bag stuffed with cash around her belly or slip notes into her socks. She was swindled out of money quite a few times after asking a South Korean she didn't know too well to transfer money on her behalf to China. She also lost money by lending it to people without even getting an IOU. After the restoration of diplomatic relations in 1992, she also began to export goods to Russia through China: leather jackets, long coats, cooking oil, and lipstick, to name a few. In fact, C claims to have exported everything except highly illegal goods like weapons, drugs, or people.

C became involved in establishment of KCA in the course of business. In 1995, there was a community of Korean Chinese and Korean small traders selling small goods like batteries, medicinal products, and toothbrushes clustered around the gate of Pagoda Park in the old centre of Seoul. This was where C met Y, the KCA's future chairman, and they have been friends ever since. In 2000, things were to change as the government began a crackdown on street traders and banned them altogether on the 1st of April. However, this was not equally applied: while Korean Chinese were prohibited from trading Korean traders were still allowed to operate. Y had already acquired South Korean nationality but was still prevented from trading on the basis that she was Korean Chinese. For C, it was understandable that foreign nationals like herself might be prevented from setting up stalls on the street, but the idea that Y, a Korean national, was also unable to do business distressed her. They began to think about how they could fight for their businesses but still hadn't begun thinking about forming any kind of organization. As their situation was difficult, C and the others went looking for a church. They found uijulo church and Pastor Y, who specialized in human rights. Pastor Y was visually impaired, so he recommended they contact a pastor he knew in Incheon, Y (the future chairman) rang this pastor in Incheon, who suggested contacting Pastor L, who was based in Seoul. C's party went to meet Pastor L and was introduced by him to Pastor H. Pastor L said he couldn't properly judge the situation without listening to both sides, so he and pastor H went to visit Pagado Park. The pastors found that, as the group had told them, only Korean Chinese traders were being chased away. This was how C's group gained the support of a human rights activist in the church.

For pastor L the group's problems gave him a mission, and he worked hard to help them. His church was in a poor state, but the group moved in, cleaned, and decorated it from the ground up. It was a small church but they made it tidy and cosy. C says that she is still grateful to the pastor for helping them even though this was the best they could do for him. In 2003 and 2004, the KCA participated in a demonstration, led by the (KCWMC), demanding a change in the legal status of the Korean Chinese. The KCA's slogan was "Korean Chinese are compatriots." In 2005, they became independent from the church and set up independent dwellings in Hongje-dong. This was the exclusive activity space and the residence of the KCA. The organization's membership fee was initially 5,000 won but rose to 10,000 won later.

Y, the KCA's chairman, was born in 1950 in Antu County, Jillin. In 1973, she settled in Chaoyangchuan County of Longjing City. This was a rural area, and she married a man from a poor family – life was difficult. They had nothing soft to put in a quilt, let alone anything made of cotton. She made bedclothes from pieces of blanket. As part of the Chinese economic reform of 1980 the government said they would be dividing and distributing land. But Y couldn't live only by farming, so she jumped into business selling wardrobes. She had children and when they were sick the medical bills were expensive. Life got a little better after the reforms and the start of her business. Other households were the same – the men farmed and women started businesses. Like everyone else she began to trade clothes – buying them from the city and selling them in the countryside. She travelled to Changchun, Shenyang, Dalian, Qingdao to get stock, and later, when the business was going well, even went as far as Fuzhou and Xiamen in southern China.

In Yanbian and the surrounding region in 1988 and 1989 trade with North Korea was in full swing, and the clothes Y imported from southern China were even exported to North Korea. When North Korean products came in, they were distributed to other regions through her. In 1990, she began trade with people in the Soviet Union (Russia), travelling to Khabarovsk and selling Chinese light industry products in 1991. However, the financial difficulties at home didn't fundamentally improve. To make matters worse, her husband had a stroke and they had to pay many hospital bills. Moving to South Korea could solve all their financial problems at once. And this is what she did in April 1994 (fake marriage to South Korean man). She had to pay 50,000 yuan for the trip to Korea, but because she came through marriage, she was able to obtain Korean nationality. To pay her debts she worked in various fields, but it was difficult because it was not what she had done before. She went back to the thing she found most familiar – business.

However, as we heard in C's account, in 2000 street merchants were banned and Korean Chinese traders found themselves being moved on by the authorities while Korean nationals were left alone. Y had obtained Korean nationality, but this still didn't prevent her from facing the same treatment dealt out to other traders born in China. Her parents were all born in Chungcheongnam-do, and she had come back to her parents' home country and even acquired South Korean nationality, but she was still included in the regulations. Y recounts that somebody contacted the Foreign Worker Centre (a kind of NGO) and went to talk to them but didn't receive much help. This was when she got in touch with a pastor in Incheon, and it was through him that she came to know pastor H and pastor L. Pastor H and pastor L put a lot of effort into helping her and her group. They visited the area themselves and spoke to the local officials on her behalf. The local officials said that it was not Korean Chinese who were being targeted specifically but rather that Korean Chinese street vendors were being moved on as a consequence of general maintenance. Y, though, was finding that she didn't even have time to lay out her goods before being moved on. H pastor said that Korean-Japanese or Korean-American wouldn't be treated like this and suggested that since there were nearly 200,000 Korean Chinese they should unite together. At this point Y had also been thinking about getting some people together to see what they could do about their situation, so C gathered six people from the Pagoda Park street vender community and they all had dinner with pastor H. Y says that when there is a get-together, it has to have a name, and they decided to call theirs the "Korean Chinese Association". There also needs to be a president and a secretary, and Y had South Korean citizenship, so she became the president. C, who had led the meeting, became the secretary.

Pastor H recommended that the gatherings continue and that they try to attract more people, so Y and the others walked around with fliers explaining to people in similar situations as themselves why Korean Chinese should to band together. As well as their own patch, they also visited Cheonggyecheon and the area around Seoul station, but no one else was interested in joining. That meant there were only six people in the early meetings. Each person paid 5,000 won each, making a total of 30,000 won. Before meeting Y's group, pastor L had been working to help Korean Chinese who had been swindled by Korean nationals. As part of this, she and her group washed second-hand clothes that they then sent to China or sold at Tapgol Park. The proceeds went towards providing scholarships to the children of fraud victims. This project was the first thing that the newly formed association became involved in. Within six months of their establishment on April 4th, 2000 their membership expanded to 18, including 12 Chinese nationals and six South Korean nationals.

The KCWMC was established on the 15th of October 2000. Korean Chinese people started to gather together, and the KCA and the KCWMC working together helped to bring even more people into the fold. However, Y and the others did not know much about Christianity, thinking of it as akin to superstition. But with Pastor Y working so hard on their behalf, they felt no choice but to participate in church activities. By late 2000, the KCA had subsidiaries under its umbrella and no less than 12 executives. It boasted a president, vice president, general affairs manager, accountant, organizational manager, and "daily life manager". On the 31st of December 2000, Y and C opened a preparatory committee for the KCA and set out the society's regulation in a seven-page document. The association did not work alone, but with other churches with common agendas.

From 2001, the legal issue regarding Overseas Koreans Act began to surface. The pastor in charge said that he needed to campaign for the revision of the Overseas Koreans Act and advised Y to stop business activities. This wasn't easy because while Y had saved money every month, the long disruption to her business had forced her to use all her savings. To make matters worse her Chinese husband passed away in 2003. By the time the Overseas Koreans Act was finally amended, Y herself had already become penniless. Talking about why she chose to become so involved in the movement, she reflected,

> I did not do this because I'm a red [left-winger]. What does a farm-er's wife who came to Korea to eat, live and make money for her family know of politics? I was fated to try it and fell in deep.

In sum, from 2001 the KCA has been organizing meetings to pursue revision of the Overseas Koreans Act, the abolishment of the foreign training system and establishment of a work permit system, praying for the forced deportation, crucifix, and revision of the Overseas Koreans Act, and were vocal about almost every issue affecting Korean Chinese (KCA 2010).

The above account shows us that the first Korean Chinese organization had merchants at its centre and formed with the help of the church. In a situation where the legal status of the Korean Chinese was unstable, the church provided them, not only with shelter but also with the reasoning and sense of legitimacy that they needed to throw themselves into campaigning. This meant that in the early days the KCA were acting according to the logic of a religious organization rather than their own. Religious groups led the campaign to revise the OKA, and the KCA followed their lead.

Organizations with entrepreneurs at their core

The first group organized by business people in the Korean Chinese enclave was the Korean Compatriot Merchant Association (KCMA, *jaehandongposang-inhoe*). This was formed in 2006 to help Korean Chinese entrepreneurs based in Garibong-dong share information between themselves. Its founder is K, the president of J Noodles. K was born in 1955 in Longjing City, Jilin Province, and is highly educated. After graduating from high school in 1972, she moved to the countryside and worked on weather observation. She then began to work in publishing after being recommended to a state-owned publishing company by a textbook compilation committee member. She was able to enter university without taking the entrance examination and when she graduated began to work at a research institute. She went to Beijing in 1992 and did translation work, mainly for Korean businessmen looking to expand into China, for two years. After that K returned to Yanbian and started a pharmaceutical company (a move that was easier for her because many of her relatives worked in this field). This background provided K with experience working as a professional and owning a business in China.

In 1997, K came to South Korea and started her noodle restaurant business. She initially started this in Wangsimni but soon moved it to Garibong-dong. It was a success from the beginning, perhaps, as she suggests, because when she worked in Beijing, she also studied at an economics college and the things she learnt there helped a great deal. Whatever the reason, K started to make really make her mark the following year, opening four more branches in areas like Ansan and Gasan Digital Complex where there were a lot of Korean Chinese residents. The original Garibong-dong branch continued to grow too, and K has become the very image of a successful Korean Chinese entrepreneur. It was during this period of growth that the editor-in-chief of the KCTN (Mr K) suggested to K that the areas successful business people should form a business council.

Although she didn't think of the idea herself, K was convinced that the editor's suggestion needed to be implemented. From 9 March 2006, she began to visit the local business owners to discuss whether they would like to participate. Three months later, 84 representatives from 84 different companies gathered for the first meeting of the business council at the KCTN's office. Most of the Korean Chinese business owners who participated in the formation of the association, including President K himself, had stabilized their legal status in the country by acquiring nationality. They represented 16 different types of businesses, including restaurants, karaoke room operators and travel agents, and they were able to pay 50,000 won a month for the membership fee. The business council soon became the most economically powerful non-religious organization in Korean Chinese society.

Before the business council formed there was an association for first generation Korean Chinese who had recovered Korean nationality called the Korean Returnees' Association (KRA, *gwihandong-poyeonhabhoe*). This had about 270 members with an average age of 65. It's president, W, contacted and met with K through some mutual acquaintances and asked whether K would like to run the groups together since his association's members were all elderly and had few economic resources. This was really a request to help give the KRA a new lease of life. W's proposal was accepted and on 12 November 2006, the business council and the KRA joined together to form the General Assembly of Korean Compatriots' Association (GAKCA, *jaehandongpoyeonhabconghoe*). The business council's office became the General Assembly's office. There were about 380 members at the beginning of the merger. It set up branch offices in Geumcheon, Guro, Yeongdeungpo, Ansan, and Daejeon, and ran the original business council, but also a hiking group, a football team, a volleyball team, an art society, a volunteer society, and a youth group. It came to include in its members, not just businessmen, but also various groups from Korean Chinese society. At first, the group used the term "association" and, as a point of principle, tried to make decisions big and small through the board of directors. But, in practice, it found that decisions began to be made by a small group centred on the president.

In 2015, the GAKCA became a corporation and was registered as a nonprofit organization with the Ministry of Foreign Affairs and Trade (General Assembly of Korean Compatriots' Association 2015). Its structure was also reorganized to meet the requirements of being a corporate body and the role of its affiliated organizations were made clearer. It was now one of the principal organizations representing Korean Chinese society in the enclave. It's founding goal was to "contribute to the stable settlement and development of compatriots within South Korea and to encourage their harmony growth through exchanges with Korean compatriot organization overseas" (Article 3 of the organization's institution).

The United Association of Korean Chinese (UAKC, *junggugdong-pohanmaeumhyeobhoe*) appeared at the same time as the GAKCA and was also shaped around a core of Korean Chinese entrepreneurs. Despite starting as a sports club, it developed into another of the social organizations that played a key role in representing the enclave's Korean Chinese community. L, the owner of S Lamb Skewer in Daelim-dong, led its formation.

Born in Heilongjiang province's Mishan, L moved to Dunhua City in Jilin province when he was 10 years old. This is where he grew up, met his wife (who went to the same school as him), and started a family. He says he couldn't stay in school as long as he wanted, but after graduating secondary school he spent two to three years teaching at an elementary school. His wife worked as a hospital nurse, so while there was just the two of them, they were able to manage financially. However, after they had a child, life was harder to get by. A lot of people they knew were going to live abroad, and they decided that this would be best for them too. They choose Korea because they could both speak the language. They arrived in Korea in 1997, and he began work in Shihwa Industrial Complex in Ansan. But, just a day and a half after starting work, he had an accident and severed his right arm. He had only been in the country for three days. He ended up being treated in South Korea before going visiting China for further treatment. Now he was disabled, however, he wasn't able to find a job. Luckily, he had the chance to take over a small, four-table lamb skewer restaurant in Doksan-dong. His business grew, and he moved to Daerim-dong, where it grew even more. He began a second business, this time specializing in Chinese hotpot.

In 2006, L started a small soccer get-together. As this grew into a soccer team, more and more people started to join. At this time, someone inside the soccer team suggested doing volunteer work as well as soccer. A volunteer society was formed and service began. The small groups like the soccer team and volunteer group became active and led to the establishment of the UAKC at the end of 2008. By this time, there was one volunteering group, one football team, one volleyball team, and one hiking group. The group, which has a relatively young membership, elects presidents for two-year terms. After L, the next president was M, the owner of L Corporation. K became its third president in 2015. The association has a formal and systematic organization that is expressed in its constitution (UAKC 2012).

According to its constitution,

> based on the universal value of humanity required in the era of globalization, the organization supports our precious 'national wealth' of 7 million Korean compatriots by helping to form an 'ethnic network' and through this to support the development of a mature compatriot Korean society. As such the main purpose of this project is to establish non-profit public service projects that will lay the foundation for utilizing global talents and strengthening national education. The association will strive to strengthen cooperation between the Koreas and enhance the nations' dignity by fostering cultural diplomacy. It will look to by strengthening the status of global Korea and support human resource exchange. It will thus strive for the improvement, development and growth of the nation"
>
> (Article 3 of association, UAKC 29 October 2009, 2012)

A third body led by business owners was founded in 2015. This was formed by its Korean Chinese members to properly prepare for their participation in a public consultation on issues surrounding Korean Chinese in Seoul (this consultation was called "Southwest Seoul's Public Consultation for Resolving the Problems of Korean Chinese"). The meeting was proposed by L, a Korean Chinese woman who was at that time serving as the honorary deputy mayor of Seoul City. The rationale behind setting up this kind of meeting was "the need to establish a meeting where Korean Chinese people who are participating in the public consultation could discuss current issues, and create and agree on proposals." This meeting gave birth to the Korean Chinese Committee (KCC, *junggugdongpowiwonhoe*). The meetings were attended by representatives from Korean Chinese organizations and newspapers. These attendees included J, president of the Multicultural Sports Federation; K, the chairman of the Korean Chinese Society Institute; P, president of the CK Women's Committee; J, chairman of Korea-China Foundation; M, principal of Eoulim Weekend School: K, representative of the Korea China Business Newspaper; K, editor of the Northeast Asia Newspaper; L, editor of Korean branch of Heungyongang Newspaper; K, editor-in-chief of the Gilim Newspaper; C, president of the Hanminjok Newspaper; Y, Geumcheon branch president of Korean Chinese Association General Assembly; P, the secretary general of the Korean Chinese Literary Society; K, the former president of the GAKCA; H, secretary general of the Korea-China International Trade Association; M, editor-in-chief of the Hanjungdongpo Newspaper; K, a representative of the Korean Chinese Multicultural Clean Environment Volunteering Group, and J, chairman of the preparatory committee for Korean Chinese Public Services Community (DBA News 24 March 2015).

The delegates were almost all business people. Some were there on behalf of their businesses and some were representing an organization they participated in during their spare time. A preparatory committee was formed. At its centre was L from Seoul city, K from the Korea-China International Trade Association, J from the Korean Chinese Permanent Resident Association, and P from the CK Women's Committee. In the course of eleven preparatory meetings, they met Korean Chinese groups from all different occupations and classes. They explained the necessity, effectiveness, and purpose of establishing the association and were able to gain support. They even attracted support from professionals – a group that wasn't generally interested in the various issues affecting Korean Chinese Society – since, from the beginning, the association included entrepreneurs who had been foreign students in the past. The networks of these former students connected the group to Korean Chinese in professional occupations.

The associations' preparations were completed in about six months. From 11 November 2015 to 6 October 2015, the committee members and the standing committee candidates were registered, and there were elections on November 8. There were eight candidates in all – representatives from Hanminjok Newspaper (J), the Korea-China International Trade Association (K) and Chungwon International (K), academics from Hongik University (J) and Liaoning University (S), the president of Chinese Art and Calligraphy Association (L), and the directors of JMS World Travel Agency (J) and Daelim International Academy (M). Of these eight candidates five were entrepreneurs. J, the representative of the Hanminjok Newspaper was appointed as the standing committee chairman of the Korean Chinese Committee, and the representative of Korea-China International Trade Association, K, was elected as the senior vice chairman. The other candidates were all elected to be standing committee members. The Korean Chinese Committee thus became another business owner-oriented organization.

In his inaugural greeting, Chairman J emphasized that "the Korean Chinese Committee was the first organization to emerge through democratic elections in the Korean Chinese community". He further stressed the fairness and legitimacy of the procedures and highlighted the various classes and professions represented among its members.

At the 11th meeting of the preparatory committee, the attendees constantly emphasized democracy and democratic institutions. Chairman J said,

> I will contribute to helping Korean Chinese settle in Korea, to harmonize themselves, to share information, to lead each other and to enhance the image of Korean Chinese society ... there are many people in Korea who are shining like jewels – professors, lawyers, journalists, PhDs, activists, model citizens, leaders of organizations, corporate heads and government officials. And yet, Korean Chinese are still viewed negatively in South Korea ... In order to improve this image, we have established an organized system that will maintain itself. If we act as a focal point, gathering the efforts of our community, we can identify the issues affecting the community, formulate countermeasures, and implement change. I expect that the resulting transformation of Korean Chinese society will gain us the respect of South Koreans.[1]

By this, chairman J meant that elites should take the lead and improve the negative aspects of Korean Chinese society.

The KCC established its constitution to define the character and structure of the organization (KCC 2016). They stated that the committee's purpose was to "contribute to the harmonization and co-prosperity of the Korean and Korean Chinese and the Korean communities by setting up a committee system that could channel the efforts of the Korean Chinese community and pursue their goals". In addition,

> it will contribute to the harmonization and development of the Korean Chinese and wider local communities by acting as a point of exchange and contact between the South Korean government, South Korean society and Korean Chinese communities, and as a bridge for economic, cultural and social exchanges between China and South Korea. It will thus help raise the status of the Korean Chinese community.
>
> (Article 2 of the Constitution)

Defining their key values as democracy, public interest, and self-reliance led the committee to "build a democratic and fairly organizational system, implement public interest projects for Korean Chinese, and seek to establish the self-sufficiency and wisdom required for sustainable development" (Article 3 of the Constitution).

Organizations for entrepreneurs

In 2013, the UAKC was being sponsored by a public corporation and operating the Korean Chinese Entrepreneurial Academy. A total of 280 students attended the academy, which was run in three stages and had a constant stream of new students every term. The academy focused on entrepreneurship, management, trade, commerce, commercial law, tax law, and FTA rules. It invited professionals to come and talk about economic issues and share some of their experiences in business. And was received by the Korean Chinese community extremely positively. People who were either planning a start-up or already running their own business attended it enthusiastically, and no one in the association had expected just how positive the reaction would be.

K, the vice chairman of the Korea-China Entrepreneurship and Management Association (KCEMA, *hanjungcangeobgyeongyeonghyobhoe*), reflected,

> The Korean Chinese community in Korea has been changing rapidly since about 2007 or 2008 because members of the elite and business owners are now free to stay in Korea permanently. These were not just simple laborers, but people from various different classes group of people who could now stay and demonstrate their abilities. Moreover, as Korea's relationship with China became closer, Korean Chinese found themselves with some degree of legal status, entrepreneurship, ability and capital stemming from this relationship. Of course, this was still all at an early stage. So I thought we needed to have a qualitative leap forward in the Korean society and for that I believed that an economic association was necessary. The students also had a great deal of interest in this area.
>
> (K, vice chairman of the KCEMA)

The idea of establishing the KCEMA came from the key leaders of the UAKC. At the time this was Chairman L, Vice Chairman K, Secretary M, and General Secretary L. These people were not only managing their own businesses but also establishing a trading company. Because they were young entrepreneurs, they had a lot of passion, desire for success, and a strong sense of responsibility. And as they were both being entrepreneurs and running the United Association, they were able to quickly grasp the entrepreneurial atmosphere of Korean Chinese society and respond with projects like the academy.

The KCEMA actually began life on a mobile community application called "N-band", which was popular with smartphone users in South Korea. Soon, some members suggested that they form an official offline organization, and the "Korean Chinese Entrepreneurship Association" had been discussed as a possible name before they finally decided on the "Korea-China Entrepreneurship and Management Association". The group's inauguration, held in March of 2014 at the Seoul Global Center, was attended by about 200 people, including representatives from China's Commerce Department, Seoul City Hall, Chinese and Korean economic organizations, media companies, and other Korean Chinese organizations. Within one year of its foundation, the organization had more than 967 online members.

In his opening address, K, the KECMA's first president and the owner of H Travel Agency, observed that

> as the economic strength of Korean Chinese is growing, the number of people who have started businesses or are thinking of doing so is increasing. To increase overall prosperity, the association will play a key role in stimulating economic exchange between Korean and China by setting up programmes aimed at potential Korean Chinese entrepreneurs, business owners, Koreans entrepreneurs with China-related businesses and Chinese entrepreneurs with Korean-related businesses.

The vice chairman, K (who was also the executive vice president of the UAKC), developed this theme and stressed how necessary the new association was:

> 900,000 Chinese nationals are long-term residents here, 4 million Chinese tourists visit every year, and 80,000 Koreans studying or working in China. The Korea-China FTA has nearly been agreed, and the economic and cultural exchanges between Korea and China are at an unprecedented level ... the stabilization of legal status and resulting long-term residence of entire families, improving financial power, and the mass influx of young people has led to the rapid growth of Korean Chinese society. This, in turn, has produced a significant increase in the number of Korean Chinese who have left their jobs and are now starting up businesses. There are more than 5,000 Korean Chinese stores in the country, and other industries such as trade, consulting, tourism, and distribution are growing rapidly. In this context the association runs educational and academic activities related to entrepreneurship and

management. These activities help to expand the economic opportunities available to Korean Chinese and Koreans and Chinese people who run, or are looking to start, businesses related to trade between Korea and China.

(*Jungugdongposhinmun* 25 March 2014)

The KCEMA was composed of professional business people and its main purpose was to contribute to economic prosperity. In early 2016, the association appointed its second, and very young, executive team. S (from M joint-stock corporation) was appointed chairman; K (the chairman of the UAKC) became advisory chairperson. The former chairperson of the UAKC became a vice chairperson along with L (1), H, and L (2). P became secretary-general, and L was appointed as director of operations.

The organization was structured according to article 40; subsection 2 of their statutes. They aimed to,

expand the economic opportunities available to Korean Chinese and Koreans and Chinese people who run, or are looking to start, businesses related to trade between Korea and China by running free education and academic activities related to entrepreneurship and management.

(KCEMA 2014)

Shortly after the establishment of the KCEMA, K, the senior vice chairman of the association, said, "I felt limited because we were only working with people who wanted to start a new business and not the newly-formed group of Korean Chinese business people". The newly formed group K meant were people engaged in trade between China and Korea, and they had considerable purchasing power. K and other key Pictures decided that

we needed an organization for these people. I thought that these people are like a bridge between traders and buyers and that they play a definite role when small or medium-sized Korean enterprises look to enter the Chinese market. I also thought that they would surely contribute to South Korea's economy by attracting investment from China. For this purpose, we organized was the Trade Association and set up sub-committees for different industries and sectors. We are also forming subcommittees for different cities in both China and Korea.

(Interview of K)

The new Korea-China Trade Association (KCTA, *hanjungmuye-oghyeobhoe*) was established on 24 December 2014. K became the chairman, K, the senior vice president and K, J, P, S were all made executive vice presidents. S was given the role of secretary general. This association too, had an official constitution that shaped its goals and form:

> The Association is engaged in educational and academic activities related to the Korea-China FTA, trade and cultural goods. Moreover, by our members' commitment to friendship it will promote goodwill, economic exchange and opportunity for Chinese, Korean, and Korean Chinese traders and buyers engaged in trade between the two countries.
>
> (KCTA 29 November 2014)

In addition to the trade association, there are also two more organizations, the CK Women's Committee and the Central Korean Chinese Assembly (CKCA). The former is chaired by P, the owner of K Travel Agency, and concentrates on women's meetings. The latter is chaired by K from Y Noodles and has been expanding its influence in the enclave through special events.

Summary

In the late 1980s and early 1990s, the church led efforts to secure the legal status of Korean Chinese and organized the first Korean Chinese merchant organization. After the legal status of the Korean Chinese people was stabilized, groups led by entrepreneurs appeared. As the leading group emerging from the enclave, the entrepreneur groups paid attention to the enclave's size, character, the perception that outsiders had of it, and the government policies concerning it. After all, the existence of an enclave was directly related to their own existence. The entrepreneurs were aware of the need to preserve the enclave, and this understanding became the logical basis for their active citizenship practices.

Note

1 Refer to the home page of the Korean Chinese Committee, http://koreadp. korean.net/bbs/content.php?co_id=greeting.

References

DBA News. 24 March 2015. "To Create Korean Chinese Consultative Body before the Establishment of the Southwest Seoul's Government-Public Consultation for Resolving the Problems of Korean Chinese" (in Korean).

General Assembly of Korean Compatriots' Association. 2015. *Articles of Association* (in Korean). Seoul.

Jungugdongposhinmun. 25 March 2014. "Korean Chinese Economic Organizations Create Korea-China Entrepreneurship and Management Association" (in Korean).

Korean Chinese Association. 2010. *10th Anniversary of Korean Chinese Association* (in Korean).

Korean Chinese Committee. 2016. (http://koreadp.korean.net) (in Korean). Seoul.

Korean Chinese Committee. 24 January 2016. *Article of Association* (in Korean).

Korea-China Entrepreneurship and Management Association. 9 February 2014. *Article of Association* (in Korean). Seoul.

Korea-China Trade Association. 29 November 2014. *Article of Association* (in Korean).

Kukmin Ilbo. 18 October 2000. "Korean Chinese Welfare Mission Center Opening" (in Korean). 17th page.

United Association of Korean Chinese. 28 October 2009. *Introduction to United Volunteer Service* (in Korean). Seoul.

United Association of Korean Chinese. 2012. *Articles of Association* (in Korean). Seoul.

6 Identity

Seeing impartiality

Seeing social equity

The enclave's business community was calling for a "special law" for ethnic Koreans living in the country without South Korean citizenship. They recognized that the Overseas Koreans Act had played an important role integrating Korean Chinese into South Korean society by giving more Korean Chinese the chance to change their legal status. But they saw that because the Overseas Koreans Act was aimed at ethnic Koreans living abroad, it did not specifically cover Korean Chinese who were living in South Korea. That made it an insufficient basis for policies impacting on the Korean Chinese community living in the country. The entrepreneurs argued that "Currently, there are more than 600,000 Korean Chinese [living in South Korea] and that's not including ethnic Koreans with other nationalities. But they are all, in fact, in a legal blind spot". Chairman K emphasized that

> If one acquires South Korean nationality there are rights and obligations. The cases of women who have come to the country through marriage are covered included by the 'Multicultural Family Support Act'. But the group excluded from both of these categories is ethnic Koreans with foreign citizenship like Korean Chinese.
>
> (Korea-China Trade Association [KCTA], Chairman K)

The term "special law" had been circulating for a long time in politics and the media. An early example is to be found from the media coverage of the "Seminar on Policies Promoting Early Adaptation by Compatriots who have Acquired Citizenship". This was held on 18

June 2010 and was chaired by a congressman from the Hannara Party (congressman J). *Yonhap* News's K, reflecting on the proceedings, argued that "In order to maintain stable policies, it is necessary to support vocational education and employment services". He believed that "it is necessary to enact a special law for the Korean Chinese who have acquired citizenship" (DBA News 19 June 2010).

There were also occasional references to a "special law" in political circles, too. During the 2012 presidential election, there was a public declaration of support for candidate P from some Korean Chinese who had acquired citizenship. In return, the general manager of the Saenuri Party's headquarters, K, stated,

> The Saenuri Party has decided to enact special laws and decrees to improve the treatment of Korean Chinese with and without citizenship. We will pay more attention to the issue and take positive actions, such as establishing a department dedicated to planning and carrying out related tasks.
>
> (Asia News 25 November 2012)

The term "special law" by famous politicians were being re-established active demands by the leaders of Korean Chinese associations. These demands were for laws that would apply, not only to ethic Koreans who had already "reclaimed" South Korean nationality, but also to ethnic Koreans in a variety of legal positions, including "Foreign Korean Workers" and permanent residents.

Chairman K said that "The establishment of this 'special law' will require the government to establish dedicated departments responsible for matters related to Korean Chinese". That means K was demanding both specialized laws and departments. And this was not all. He further argued that there needed to be a dedicated Korean Chinese budget:

> There is nowhere where we can register as a compatriot organization. There is no department and no budget. It is not that Korean Chinese are not 'multicultural', but that when we get down to a practical level, there is nothing in common between 'multicultural' issues and the issues that affect Korean Chinese. If we want to hold an amateur singing contest for Korean Chinese in Daelim-dong, the government has no funding. If we say that it is a multicultural singing contest then we can get funding.
>
> (KCTA, Chairman K)

K said,

> in Seoul there are schemes aimed at Korean Chinese, and I think they are very important. For example, through 'Southwest Seoul's Public Consultation for Resolving the Problems of Korean Chinese' our association worked with the director of the Immigration Office, national assembly members, city councillors, local councillors and Korean Chinese community representatives to develop programmes on public order, education, culture and social integration. And we would like to do more. But is there funding for this kind of association? Solving problems as they come up is good, but in the end there needs to be a special law. The budget, proper departments, and which officials are responsible must be determined through a special law.

The entrepreneurs saw that local authorities were not able set up policies or programmes for Korean Chinese because there was neither a specific law nor a specific department to do so. They said that these institution problems made it impossible to manage and fund events set up by Korean Chinese organizations. At one conference in July, 2013, the entrepreneurs complained that

> South Korea's multicultural budget is 280 billion KRW, and the budget allocated to Korean Chinese is 10 million KRW. This is not enough support to give to the community who make up half of all foreign residents. There are 580,000 Korean Chinese living in Korea, but their living conditions are poor. There must be a dedicated department in the government and continual communication with Korean Chinese society.
>
> (Yang and Park et al. 2013: 169–170)

Chairman L reflected,

> If you are like me, you can live, and live very well. Although there are no big obstacles to living in Korea, from the perspective of Korean Chinese, the way the government continues to treat foreigners is regrettable. On May 3, 2009, we held the first United Athletic Meet for Korean Chinese. There has never been a nationwide meet like this that was organized by a small private organization before. 16 soccer teams attended. In the case of the Republic of Korea, this kind of event was held by a small private organization. We went to the Overseas Koreans Foundation to ask for help, but they said that

they support ethnic Koreans who are abroad, and not those who are in the country. So I personally spent 30 million won, and it was very tough. It is the same now. In fact, with emergence of multiculturalism Korean Chinese issues have been in the background for a long time. Looking at the budget, there is almost nothing for Korean Chinese. They say that this is the era of 1.2 million foreigners, and that's just comical. Us Korean Chinese account for more than 400,000 of that Picture, but even though they include Korean Chinese who have the same bloodline [in the Pictures for multicultural] but there are no measures and no money. It's so sad.

(Park and Kim et al., 2012: 234–235)

Seeing stigmatization

Chairman K of the KCTA commented,

Local governments need to support events that improve the capability of Korean Chinese, develop initiatives to improve social integration, and create programmes that expand the opportunities for Korean Chinese. The most important of these are civic and citizenship education projects. I think education about law and order for all foreigners, not just Korean Chinese is urgent. Community conflicts are actually sparked by trivial things. In the case of improper garbage disposal – in China the government takes charge of the separation and collection of garbage once you pay a sanitation fee. People had problems when they came to Korea because they didn't understand the system at all. Neither the state nor the local administration pays any attention to these issues but the press will make special mention of the problems they cause. In general, we need to spend money on education. Preventing a problem is cheaper than treating one.

While there was absolutely no effort put into policies to promote the integration of Korean Chinese and harmony in the enclave, whenever there was a problem all focus was turned on the stigmatized enclave Korean Chinese. The businessmen were actually hoping for a selective welfare policy: "It is important to focus on the education of the elderly, children, middle-income children, and opportunities for ordinary adults, as well as opportunities for economic activities such as employment and start-ups", emphasized Chairman K. But the Korean government's immigration policy was referred to as a "support policy", and worst of all, Korean Chinese were looked down on as a group that took from South Korea without giving anything back.

Group activities

Activities emphasizing the character of ethnic compatriot Koreans

The General Assembly of Korean Compatriots' Association (GAKCA) believed that educational activities were most important. From 2011, they ran monthly Korean history courses for Korean Chinese. Chairman K said,

> Even though Korean Chinese have studied history in China, there is a lot they do not know about our Korean history and culture. We went to the History Museums, of course, but just looking doesn't provide much depth. Last year, we had history lessons on the third Tuesday of every month. Professors from Seoul National University gave free two-hour lectures.
>
> (Park and Kim et al., 2012: 344)

The general assembly regarded the proactive pursuit of knowledge about Korean history and culture to be important for adapting to Korean society.

The United Association of Korean Chinese (UAKC) and the KCTA have jointly visited historical and cultural events since 2015. The event programme is subtitled "A Holiday to Find Myself", and it is claimed that

> through field trips and education about Korean history and national cultural history Korean Chinese will learn about their national lineage and roots, be inspired with a sense of historical identification and national pride, and discover our future vision and role through the "Korean Dream".

K, the event's organizer and the chairman of the KCTA, emphasized that he thought that

> Korean Chinese think of Korean history as a condition for settling in the country. As for any country, history knowledge is required to understand the culture and society. In the future, this kind of

business will proceed steadily and the route will be diversified so that as many people as possible can understand the history and culture of Korea.

(KCTA, Chairman K)

These educational activities were still being promoted as of 2019. And these associations also sought to inform Koreans about the history of Korean Chinese migration.

A large number of Korean Chinese groups, led by the UAKC, have been holding a "Korean Chinese Migration History Painting and Photo Exhibition" in Daelim-dong Garibong-dong since 2015. The event is subtitled, "Making a village festival through cultural communication between Korean Chinese and local residents." By holding the exhibition on Korean Chinese immigration history in the enclave they tried to introduce local residents to the history and culture of Korean Chinese people and build a community based on mutual understanding and respect. Cultural and artistic activities of all sizes were being held constantly in the enclave. Most of the events aimed at fostering harmony in the local area were cultural and artistic activities. Since different groups organized these events so their content differed, but all sought to display Korean Chinese traditions.

The traditional cultural arts activities culminated in the Korean Chinese folk culture festival held for Chuseok by the Central Korean Chinese Assembly on 7 July 2014 at Yeouido Park in Seoul. Before the festival officially began the organizer said that the festival was being held to "… comfort the many Korean Chinese who cannot pay respects at their ancestors graves in China by allowing them to gather here in their homeland and do the rites together". In the morning traditional games like wrestling, Korean Chess, *yut, neolttwigi*, pitch-pot, and tug-of-war were held, and in the afternoon there was a singing contest hosted by the famous TV presenter, Song Hae. The festival event was attended by more than 20,000 people and K, the chairman of the CKCA, announced, "Every year, we will organize various traditional folklore events to improve the quality of our lives by reviving our own folk culture. We will create an opportunity for the people to unite" (DBA News 9 September 2014).

The second Korean Chinese folk culture festival was held in 2015. This event, too, began with people paying respect to their ancestors. Hosts, members, and guests came up to the podium on behalf of those who could not return home "in order to pray for the ancestors' happiness in the other world and their blessing, and also to pray for the health and happiness of the family." In his opening address, Chairman

K said that "the CKCA, with its slogan of 'Love, harmony, sharing, and hope' will do its best to create a place sympathetic to the development of cultural exchange and unity with the locals" (DBA News 27 September 2015). There were Korean traditional folk games and artistic events, and, as in 2014, it was held in Yeouido Park and attracted many Korean Chinese. It was considered a big success.

Activities for local harmony

The UAKC considered community service to be one its main responsibilities. They had established the United Volunteer Service (UVS) to do regular volunteering (UAKC 2009), and considered itself to be "one of the first to contribute to the creation of a volunteerism and donation culture in the Korean Chinese society" and sought to "help struggling Korean Chinese and disadvantaged locals". It ran various charitable activities, including fund raising and volunteering, with a goal to "improve life quality and satisfaction by teaching the spirit of service – that even small acts in the context of life in Korea conveys love to our neighbors and returns the love to us with joy". The UVS's activities included volunteer cleaning, free lunches, and volunteer centre activities that were run at least once a month (UAKC 2009). They regularly ran clean-up drives in the enclave, and in winter collected donations to provide impoverished residents with rice or fuel. These and other systematic volunteer service activities were the main endeavour of the United Association.

The GAKCA established its Gamcheon branch in 2010. This branch was the only centre for Korean Chinese senior citizens approved by the Ward Office, which supported it with 200,000 won every month. Elderly people from other areas began to come use these facilities and caused inconvenience for existing users, so in April 2010, the GAKCA established another centre for senior citizens in Guro that had facilities for around 60 elderly users. In the same year the group began running a shelter for Korean Chinese. This was opened because from 2010 Korean Chinese without relatives in the country began to enter with C-3 visas. These people couldn't stay with relative and because they were working in a foreign country and were only looking for somewhere where they could keep their luggage. At first, Chairman K used his restaurant as a shelter, but this was inconvenient for everybody. "I thought that wouldn't do, so I decided to set up a place where these people could stay until they found a job" (Park and Kim et al. 2012: 342). This shelter was operated by the president himself – not with association funding. It was located on the first and second floor of a building and required a deposit of 20 million won and 1.2 million won a-month in rent.

While many Korean Chinese organizations wanted to operate facilitates for elderly Korean Chinese, the only group that actually put this into practice was the GAKCA. This group, which was established by President K, had a particular connection to elderly Korean Chinese people because they it was formed through an amalgamation of the Korean Compatriot Merchant Association (KCMA) with the Korean Returnees' Association (KRA), and the latter had always had an elderly membership. The centre was not just a place for its members to take a rest. This association regularly cleaned the streets and had volunteers working to improve the local environment – and members of the senior citizen's centre participated too. Although the centre was a place for them to rest, they thought image of the Korean Chinese group would improve if they served the local community. So the association organized things and made it mandatory for elderly who used the branch to do one week of voluntary work a month. "The senior citizens actually preferred it that way" (Park and Kim et al. 2012: 345).

Activities to build business networks

We have already seen that the Korea-China Entrepreneurship and Management Association (KCEMA) was launched at the end of 2013, mainly with students from the "Establishment Academy for Korean Chinese Entrepreneurs". It continued to run the academy, sharing knowledge and instructing Korean Chinese people who wanted to start a business. In 2015, this association began a new specialist education programme and invited lawyers with a variety of different specialties to be the instructors. Meanwhile, the KCTA was actively cooperating with government business. For example, it was selected to be one of the representatives of Korean Chinese entrepreneurs at the international trade and investment fair held in Gangwon province in 2015. That year, it also began to operate an "Academy for Korean Chinese self-reliance". This programme consisted of four courses. The first one was on FTA and trade lectures. The second one was on restaurants and franchises. The third one was on e-commerce, home shopping, and social commerce lectures. The fourth was on enterprise and the entrepreneurship. The association also invited marketing specialists to run an enterprise academy. This too, consisted of four courses: (1) "The enterprise process and practical enterprise know-how", (2) "Young Entrepreneurship and Successful start-ups", (3) "Cosmetics Marketing and Sales Maximization Strategy", and (4) "Successful Business

Models and Marketing Strategies". Both the KCEMA and the KCTA were established business organizations, but they actively organized business-related education programmes. The reason they actively promoted the establishment of a business network was because they identified low economic status as the initial cause of discrimination against Korean Chinese in South Korea. They believed that economic success could lead to the elimination of discrimination. The groups' names emphasized Korea and China but did not emphasize Korean Chinese ethnicity.

Given roles

The roles of representative enclave group

In 2015, the city of Seoul began a project to "strengthen the independence of Korean Chinese" as part of its social policy. The project included "Consultation on Strengthening the Educational Capacity of Korean Chinese Parents Settlement Support", and "Academy of Entrepreneurship for Korean Chinese New and Small Business owners", an "Academy and Workshop for Korean Chinese activists", and a "Korean Chinese Residents Cultural Festival" and a "Harmony Festival". Four businesses were specified as "Korean Chinese". Among these the first businesses was the KCTA, the fourth was the UAKC and the fifth was the GAKCA. The business-owner-led groups had come to be leading participants in Korean Chinese policy in Seoul City.

In addition, the report on policies related to Korean Chinese ordered by the Seoul Metropolitan City in 2013 proposed that "unlike existing multicultural policies, the positive economic, social, and cultural effects need to be expanded through policy enforcement appropriate to the characteristics of both the region and the Korean Chinese themselves." Based on this proposal, the City of Seoul is actively involved in the launch of the "Seoul Southwest Public-Private Partnership Council for Guro-gu, Geumcheon-gu, Youngdeungpo-gu and Gwanak-gu" together with members of the National Assembly, municipal councillors, related administrative agencies, and representatives of local residents (DBA News 4 March 2015). The private-public consultation body is composed of members of the National Assembly, the Seoul Metropolitan Assembly, the mayor of the Seoul Metropolitan Government, the deputy superintendent of the Seoul Metropolitan Office of Education, director of the Seoul Immigration Office, director of Guro-gu Office, director of Geumcheon-gu Office, director of Yeongdeungpo-gu Office, district governor of Gwanak-gu, Seoul Geumcheon police chief, Seoul Yeongdeungpo police chief, and Seoul Gwanak police chief. The private-public consultation body was divided into a life safety subcommittee, an education subcommittee, and a social culture subcommittee. 13 Korean Chinese representatives participated as committee members. Most of these were representatives of Korean Chinese organizations and business owners. The fact that Korean Chinese representatives are directly involved in the government-led private-public consultation and that the majority of these representatives are business owners indicates the role of business owner-led groups in Korean Chinese society. Meanwhile, politicians attended and spoke at events hosted by business owner-led organizations. This phenomenon was new. Politicians from both the ruling party and the opposition attended the Korean Chinese folk culture festival held for Chuseok by the CKCA. At the 2014 festival K from the Saenuri Party, "This Chuseok I hope to make a harmonious and cherished place to share our happiness and communicate with each other through our traditional folk games" (DBA News 9 September 2014). In 2015, Y from the Democratic Party of Korea said, "We hope that the Korean Chinese folk culture festival will continue to be held and that the 700,000 Korean Chinese residents will be united. "The Democratic Party of Korea promises to listen to the voice of Korean Chinese" (DBA News 27 September 2015).

At the New Year's meeting held in January 2015 by the Korean Chinese United Association, a member of the National Assembly made a congratulatory address (DBA News 14 January 2015). Politicians giving congratulatory addresses at the events of a group led by business owners used to be unheard of. Furthermore, during the 20th National Assembly election members in 2016, Korean Chinese entrepreneur become a representative of the Democratic Party of Korea and officially challenge the political system. Although the Entrepreneurs could not become career politicians, it was still a symbolic change for Korean Chinese society. The Democratic Party of Korea's new representative was P from Heilongjiang – the president of the K travel agency, the founder of the "CK Women's Committee", and a symbolic figure in Korean Chinese society.

The role of "elites" in Korean Chinese society

As the influence of the Korean Chinese business groups in South Korea grew, elite members of Korean Chinese society in China, including entrepreneurs, scholars, and civil servants, began to take a keen and active interest. At the Korean Chinese folk culture festival (2014) congratulatory addresses were given by P, the chairman of the Association of Korean Chinese Entrepreneurs in China, L, the chairman of the Beijing Korean Chinese Entrepreneurs Association, L, the chairman of the Guangdong Provincial Korean Chinese Association, and the chairman of the *yeonbyeon-odeogjangjuyuhan* company (also L) (DBA News 9 September 2014). Representatives of influential Korean Chinese business associations were participating in events held by Korean Chinese entrepreneur-led groups in South Korea, and attended the next year's festival too (DBA News 27 September 2015). Although there is yet to any no direct and large-scale partnerships between these Korean Chinese business owners from China and the Entrepreneurs it is meaningful that they participate in these events.

Two state-run newspapers from China, the *"Gillim* (Jilin) Newspaper"* and "The *Heugryonggang* (Heilongjiang) Newspaper", established branch offices in Korea and now regard articles on Korean Chinese in South Korea as one of their main sources of content. News about the events run by the enclave-entrepreneurs was naturally included. These newspapers companies publish separate newspapers in Korea and China, with important articles from the Korean paper also being published in China, so the role of the Entrepreneurs (or their groups) is naturally transmitted to the Korean Chinese community in China. In 2011 the Jilin Newspaper published "People Who Dreamed", a collection of success stories from Korean Chinese living in Korea. In the foreword, Jilin Newspaper's president and editor-in-chief, H, wrote,

> … There are about currently around 525,000 Korean Chinese residents living in Korea, which accounts for 1% of South Korea's population. Korean Chinese society in Korea is a part of the history of Korean Chinese in China and it is a great honor to be able to add to that history by bringing these success-stories together in one book. I would be delighted if the book could help stimulate exchange between China and Korea, and become a textbook Korean Chinese in South Korea.
>
> (*Gillim* Newspaper 2011)

The book tells 30 success-stories, and 18 of these are about entrepreneurs, which is a huge proportion for one occupation. The remaining 12 success-stories are about people who work as scholars, entertainers, or in professional jobs. The state media also saw the enclave business people as the representation of Korean Chinese in South Korea.

Korean Chinese students in Korea also had a considerable level of respect for the Entrepreneurs. The "Korean Chinese Student Network" formed in 2003 invites people from all walks of life to host an end of year ceremony. From 2010 they began to include the chairs of Korean Chinese associations on the invitation list, and they now give lectures about their current projects and how they grew their business to where they are now. In 2013, the Chinese Communist Youth League of Yanbian Korean Autonomous Prefecture established the "Yanbian Next-Generation Business Committee in Korea". The Korean Chinese Student Network hosted the event and in preparations they invited people they thought could represent Korea's Korean Chinese society – and most of these people were entrepreneurs. This suggests that younger generations who will enter into high-educated Korean Chinese or professions are also recognized as important and representative constituent groups of the Korean Chinese community. This suggests that young Korean Chinese who will become highly educated or work in professional occupations also consider the Entrepreneurs to be a key, emblematic group in the Korean Chinese community.

The entrepreneurs' role in bilateral relations between Korea and China

The Chinese Embassy was also showing a keen interest in the events hosted by the Chinese- Korean-business groups. The first Korean Chinese folk culture festival was attended by the Consulate General of the Chinese Embassy, urged Korean Chinese who were planning a long stay in Korea use the festival as a chance to "do their best for harmony with Koreans" (DBA News 9 September 2014). At the 2015 festival, the Chinese Ambassador Q attended and remarked that "Korean Chinese are the bridges and bonds connecting Korea and China", and that "We will continue to work for the wealth and prosperity of China and Korea and bilateral cooperation between the two countries" (DBA News 27 September 2015). The Chinese embassy invited representatives of influential social organizations to celebrate end-of-the-year and New Year events and hosted dinner parties. The continual participation of representatives from the Korean Chinese business community at these events indicates their position as a group thought to represent overseas Chinese society. From the standpoint of the Chinese government, the Korean Chinese entrepreneurs were successful Chinese entrepreneurs living overseas in the Republic of Korea, and the groups they led were bridges between Korea and China.

The KCTA was able to persuade a large Korean company to construct a reading room at a Chinese elementary school for free. This project was transferred to the Chinese government's Overseas Chinese Office through Korea's Overseas Chinese Association. The local government in China saw this as a contribution by successful Korean Chinese to their homeland. "The counterpart of Chinese government is Overseas Chinese Office of C City and Overseas Chinese Association" (KCTA, Chairman K). Chairman K of the KCTA was also a member of the General Assembly of the Association of Korean Residents in China and the director of the Foreign Committee of Liaoning Province.

Summary

The enclave entrepreneurs felt that the manifold negative perceptions of the enclave held in Korean society were unfair and that their own contributions to Korean society were not properly recognized. They undertook various activities aimed at changing these discriminatory perceptions and supporting the enclave. From these activities, we can see various identities held by the entrepreneurs – they were entrepreneurs, Korean Chinese, Chinese, and Korean compatriots. The entrepreneurs' reaction to the various gazes focused on the enclave created this multifaceted character. But the various roles they were asked to perform simultaneously by the states and mainstream societies of both South Korea and China maintained this diverse identity. It was this complexity that formed the identity of the enclave entrepreneurs.

References

Asia News. 25 November 2012. "Some Korean Chinese Returnees' Association Announced to Support the Presidential Candidate – Park, Geun-Hye" (in Korean).
DBA News. 19 June 2010. "It's Time to Create a "Special Law" for Returned Korean Chinese" (in Korean).
DBA News. 9 September 2014. "The 1st Korean Chinese Folk and Cultural Festival was Finished Successfully" (in Korean).
DBA News. 4 March 2015. "Southwest Seoul's Public Consultation for Resolving the Problems of Korean Chinese was Established" (in Korean).
DBA News. 27 September 2015. "The 2nd Korean Chinese Folk and Cultural Festival was Finished Successfully" (in Korean).
Gillim Newspaper. 2011. *South Korea's Korean Chinese Celebrities* (in Korean). Seoul: Joeunmunak.

Park, Woo and Yong-Sun Kim et al. 2012. *The Korea We Met: Oral History of Korean Chinese* (in Korean). Seoul: Book Korea.

United Association of Korean Chinese. 28 October 2009. *Introduction to United Volunteer Service* (in Korean).

Yang, Han-Soon and Woo Park et al. 2013. *2013 Survey of Korean Chinese Living in Seoul* (in Korean). Seoul: Seoul Metropolitan City.

7 Conclusion

China's post-socialist transformation which began at the end of 1970s was also an ideological transition in that it brought with it the idea that inequality could be tolerated in the name of development. China's Korean Chinese society was not able to escape this structural transformation and experienced rapid social and economic differentiation. While Korean Chinese who were incorporated into the leading – edge of the post-socialist society could rise into the upper class, other Korean Chinese who had experienced a decline in socio-economic status were forced to leave in search of new opportunities. The inequality born of Chinese pragmatism (or neo-liberalism) forced a population to seek new opportunities in the midst of South Korea's own unequal society (Park 2017).[1]

The period of rapid industrialization that instigated a transformation in South Korea's macro-political economy began in the 1980s. The fragmented labour market and labor supply problems that were the result of this change become a key issue for Korean society to resolve. As labour supply became a serious difficulty for small- and medium-sized businesses, they demanded that the state allow them to hire foreign labour. And because of the key roles of small- and medium-sized enterprises in almost all areas of the secondary labour market, the state relented and developed a policy of gradually introducing a foreign labour force. This policy decided the kind of labour to be employed by these small- and medium-sized businesses according to their functional role, and the state managed the nature of the available foreign labour through the visa statuses and their requirements. These citizenship policies for Foreign Workers (or migrants) have changed over time in line with economic globalization.

It was also in the 1980s that South Korea's competitive advantage over North Korea became clear, with global or regional events such as the Asian Games and the Olympics being a prime example of South

Korea boasting of their system's superiority. In this context the state began confident moves at the end of the 1980s to reconfigure their relationship with ethnic Koreans overseas, especially with those residing in communist counties. As South Korea reinstituted friendly relations with communist states one after another, Korean capital came into contact with a huge market and the ethnic Koreans from China, while CIS countries met South Korea's segmented labor market. Subsequently, the Asian financial crisis in the mid to late 1990s also fashioned a new relationship between South Korea and Overseas Koreans, and the state enacted a series of laws to allow Korean-Americans (particularly, but not exclusively) to help their mother country. South Korea's economic globalization thus came to include a kind of "(ethnic) compatriot globalization".

What implications can we derive from the South Korea's Korean Chinese entrepreneurs who emerged from this politico-economic structure?

Korean Chinese as "Foreign Workers" (*oegukinnodongja*) were gradually incorporated (in numbers limited according to the nature of the industries and the skill level of the Korean Chinese workers) into the secondary labor market according to the visa statuses made available by the state. These people's socio-economic autonomy was severely limited, and the increasing numbers of immigrant workers existing entirely outside the system exposed the limits of the system: those Korean Chinese incorporated into the secondary labor market had their freedom restricted despite existing inside the system, and those outside the system were blocked from any kind of citizenship. On the other hand, the South Korean state hoped that the newly institutionalized "Special Status of Overseas Korean (*jaeoedongpo*)" would allow groups like Overseas Koreans to contribute to the country's development (or globalization) both officially and effectively. This was when the conceptual, blood-based notions of what constituted fellow countrymen began to be made concrete in law. However, Korea's existing population of Korean Chinese in the secondary labor market was excluded from the *jaeoedongpo* status and strongly opposed this discrimination. Their effort, coupled with the constant demand for foreign industrial workers, has had a significant impact on the gradual transformation of the state's legal status of Korean Chinese (or Korean Chinese in a broad sense). However, despite this, not all Korean Chinese were allowed equal access to the *jaeoedongpo* status because the state continued to distinguish between those in the primary labor markets and the "Foreign Korean Workers (*dongponodongja*)" in the secondary labor markets. Under globalization Korea's

immigration policy has an economistic character: the nationalistic basis of policies governing overseas ethnic Korean has been adapted and
subordinated to practical industrial needs.

Human capital, social capital, and economic capital were the criteria for how effectively and efficiently Korean Chinese individuals
could contribute to specific industries, and at what level. This has had
the effect of stratifying the legal statuses of South Korea's Korean
Chinese population: holders of the Special Status of Overseas Korean
have superior socio-economic status and can change (upgrade) their
legal status by actively utilizing their resources while Korean Chinese
with Foreign Korean Worker status, with their particular skills and
function in industry, have been granted a legal status almost equivalent
to that of full South Korean citizens. In this citizenship status system
economic contribution is the primary way in which one can upgrade
one's status – the hierarchy of citizenship statuses for Korean Chinese
is a concrete reflection of the country's economistic citizenship policy.

As the potential for socio-economic freedom is proportional to legal status, Korean Chinese with overseas citizenship sought to change
their legal status (specifically, their residence status). Many transi-
tioned from Foreign Worker status to Foreign Korean Worker status,
permanent residence, Overseas Korean status, or became citizens.
The newly attained statuses provide the recipient with the freedom
to choose where to live, not just autonomy in the labor market. Unlike foreign low-skilled temporary workers who need to return to their
home country after providing labor, Korean Chinese who were able to
"upgrade" their legal status in the country could stay in South Korean
without providing labour.

Most of the Korean Chinese in South Korea had low socio-economic
status within the Korean Chinese population in China. Their legal status in South Korea was initially defined on the basis of their
socio-economic status in their home country, and they were integrated
into industries such as agriculture, manufacturing, construction, and
service industries. They functioned as low-wage and unskilled laborers, and it was difficult for them to see improve their economic status. They chose to live in areas that suit their economic level, and this
choice was linked to the stratified residential environment in South
Korea, concentrationing the population in specific areas. This spatial
congestion has led to the establishment of a Korean Chinese enclave.
This is not a closed, isolated area. People circulate in and out. Some of
the population was permanent residents working in the enclave. There
was also a mobile population that moved around Seoul and the surrounding areas. Most of the permanent population was involved in the

enclave's service industry. But the consumers were constantly flowing in and out of the area, and so the leisure activities and consumption of a diverse range of people were catered to here. It also provided services to Korean Chinese related to housing, work as well as other aspects of living in South Korea. There may seem no real reason to expect that a change in legal status would directly increase the economic status of almost all Korean Chinese. However, the new statuses guaranteed residence in their location of choice, which, in conjunction with the holder's economic status, was an important factor in the birth of an enclave populated by settled workers, temporary workers and a pool of consumers. This enclave was not formed through illegal immigration. It was the result of law and order. And it became the economic foundation of the Korean Chinese entrepreneur group class.

In addition to legal status, Korea's labor market and the resources that individual Korean Chinese were able to mobilize were factors driving the emergence of the enclave. However, it is clear that the legitimatization of the labor force living in the area allowed the establishment of formal employer-employee and production-consumption relationships. And, if legal status systematically guaranteed this relationship, the Korean Chinese population would guarantee the formalization of the businesspeople's class position. This, in turn, legitimized this group's claim to represent the area. Had a high proportion of illegal immigrants with informal employment contracts populated the enclave, the entrepreneurs would not have been able to demand to hold the status they did. In short, although legal status was not the only factor driving the concentration of Korean Chinese into the enclave, it has been a decisive factor in the emergence of a formal entrepreneur (class) within this population.

Part of the Korean Chinese population was able to do business because they actively changed their legal status and so were guaranteed residence and economic autonomy in Korea. This, along with various forms of capital, such as career history, education, family composition, and initial capital, was an important factor in the decision to begin a business.

Those with citizenship or a legal status granting equivalent rights, who also had access to resources suitable to business than other Korean Chinese became business people. Changes in legal status have ensured economic autonomy. This includes corporate ownership, residence freedom and employment. The entrepreneurs have accumulated economic wealth by utilizing their skills and various forms of capital. There are some within this community who have not been able to produce competitive businesses and who have not seen any expansion.

Nevertheless, they have still experienced changes in their economic status thanks to their business activities. They provided paid employment to the enclave's labor force, as well as employing their own family members. The formation of formal employment relations led not only to changes in the economic status of the entrepreneurs but also to the enclave's status hierarchy. The business owners were a new class group (petite bourgeoisie) that emerged from a district of unskilled and low-paid workers.

The entrepreneurs' economic activity was based on the enclave's market. These activities consisted of service businesses such as catering, distribution businesses, travel businesses, and sales businesses. Although there were variations in the size of businesses run by the entrepreneurs, the total size of the service industry catering to the enclave's population never saw any decreases. The entrepreneurs became the key group in the enclaves' service industry – the population of transitory and settled workers in the area set the scene, and the entrepreneurs became the key players. Their economic status of constructed and recognized on the basis of the enclave.

Religious groups led a series of campaigns aimed at obtaining citizenship or citizenship-equivalent statuses for Korean Chinese living in the country unlawfully or without documents that gave them security or stability. They also played a decisive role in establishing Korean Chinese associations. The first group of this type was a charitable organization formed with the help of religious organizations. We cannot say whether the small traders from this period were able to significantly expand their businesses, but it is clear that the help of religious organizations allowed them to organize themselves as they ran their businesses while without stable legal foundation in the country. The resulting associations, and the religious organizations that helped to set them up, worked to bring about the amendments to the Overseas Korean Act. The stabilization of their legal status had a significant influence on the emergence of business people as the enclave's new economic elite, and they gradually replaced religious groups as area's leaders. The business associations officially defined the fundamental requirements, such as constitutions, that the societies had to have. There were two main types of societies that entrepreneurs led: in the first entrepreneurs made up the core leadership group but were not part of the general membership. In the second business people dominated both leadership positions and the membership body. As the enclave's new leaders, entrepreneurs were forced to pay attention to the area's size, character, the opinions of outsiders on the enclave, and government policy, since their own existence was directly connected to that of the enclave. The consciousness of this connection gave birth to the groups interest in maintaining the enclave, and that became the basis for the way they practiced citizenship (their citizenship identity).

The entrepreneurs pushed activities such as (1) Korean history education and cultural arts activities that highlighted their Korean ethnicity and/or the idea of a homogeneous Korean nation. They (2) arranged volunteer activities and local festivals that promoted local harmony, and (3) built an entrepreneur network that explicitly emphasized a business-based identity. Activity (1) would not have been necessary had the South Korean state politically "recognized" their ethnic membership of the Korean nation. The policies and discussion relating to "multiculturalism" in South Korea had a strong effect on direction on policies affecting migrants and foreigners in Korea. Entrepreneurs saw their inheritance as ethnic compatriots being denied. And perceived themselves to be receiving worse treatment than "multicultural" foreigners. The Entrepreneurs organized volunteer activities, local festivals, and sporting meet-ups in order to show that the area was safe and not a negative influence on social integration. Such activities would not have been necessary the existence of the enclave was not perceived to be a problem for integration. The enclave occasionally attracted attention when there was a notable crime – regardless of whether it actually committed in the area or not. In addition, the entrepreneurs were unhappy that some people assumed that the area was riven with conflict between its Korean Chinese and Korean residents without even inquiring what people who lived there actually thought. They argue that this is a misapprehension, and that the area does not adversely affect social integration. Activities undertaken by the enclave's business class were a response Korean society unfairly singling out the enclave's Korean Chinese for problems which affect, not only other migrant groups, but even South Koreans. The entrepreneurs energetically established a network of business people. They showed of their status as successful business owners and stressed that they could play an important economic and cultural role, not only in the enclave, but also in Korea and China more widely. Again, this activity would not have been necessary if there were no negative perceptions about the economic status of the Korean Chinese population. The economic status of Korean Chinese in the enclave is thought, in popular opinion, to mean that the state will always be required to protect and support them. And it is assumed that migrants are not particularly beneficial for the economy because they send the money they earn back home. It is these public perceptions that the entrepreneurs tried to fight back against through their variation activities. They claimed that they were paying a lot of taxes, playing an important role in revitalizing the local economy, and leading economic exchanges between South Korea and China. They argued that they contributed to the state's (nation's) economic development and reduced the burden on the state by creating jobs. The entrepreneurs and their associations and groups were responding to the negative perceptions of their community that existed despite the positive contributions that they, and their associations, made in the midst of a difficult environment. The response of the entrepreneurs to these perceptions (citizenship practice) was a concrete reflection of their multifaceted identity – they were multicultural and ethnic compatriots, Chinese business people, and entrepreneurs belonging to a group with a particular economic role. And they were also (among other things) normal members of a united Korean Chinese society. Their identity (as well as their "sense of fairness" (*eogulham*)) is complex and adaptable.

Mainstream South Korean society wanted to rely on the entrepreneurs to effectively manage the enclave by establishing useful and cooperative relationships. The local administration saw that, as members of Korean Chinese society and being its core group, the entrepreneurs could be an important link between the enclave and the wider South Korean society. Mainstream Korean Chinese society in China recognized that they were the successful elite of South Korea's Korean Chinese community, and expected them to play a positive role in improving the image of Korean Chinese in Korea. The Chinese government's attention was attracted by their economic success and their growing role in South Korea. It regarded them as successful Overseas *Chinese* business people and a potentially powerful link between Korea and China. They (and perhaps the South Korean government too) expected these successful people with a Chinese background to continue actively supporting socio-economic exchanges between Korea and China, and to become a bridge between the two countries.

Because the entrepreneurs were given these roles, their citizenship practices, which were based on sense of fairness, were able to gain legitimacy, and their diverse identities were guaranteed. In other words, the identities shown in the entrepreneurs' response to negative perceptions were diverse and could be maintained and reproduced in relation to the various roles the entrepreneurs were asked to perform. They were able to comfortably reveal different identities according to the situation, and this is how their *situational* sense of fairness became possible. In practice, "*situational* sense of fairness" can be regarded as an aspect of "transformative contributory rights (transformative citizenship)", and furthermore, as a concept that can explain the identity (identities) of the entrepreneurs in terms of their role as a new group emerging from the neo-liberal transitional period. The localization of the entrepreneur's social citizenship is constituted by the interaction between their *situational* sense of fairness and the diverse roles they are asked to simultaneously perform.

Therefore, it is transformative citizenship that is the primary characteristic of the entrepreneur's identity (which we could label "rational opportunism") in South Korea's (or more widely, compressed East Asia's) neo-liberal transformation.

Note

1 This phenomenon can be seen as a part of the Globalization of Asia, or specifically, the "Asianization of Asia" (Chang 2014).

References

Chang, Kyung-Sup. 2014. "Asianization of Asia: Asia's Integrative Ascendance through a European Aperture." *European Societies* 16(3): 337–342.

Park, Woo. 2017. "Transnational Migration and Korean Chinese in Seoul" (in Korean). pp. 329–349, in *Sociology of Seoul: People, Space and Everyday Life*, edited by Seo, U-Seok, Mi-ree Byun, Baek-Yung Kim and Ji-young Kim. Seoul: Nanam.

Index

Note: **Bold** page numbers refer to tables and Page numbers followed by "n" denote endnotes.

For Product Safety Concerns and Information please contact our EU
representative GPSR@taylorandfrancis.com
Taylor & Francis Verlag GmbH, Kaufingerstraße 24, 80331 München, Germany